D1643828

WORKING DAYS

MIDLAND RED

MALCOLM KEELEY

IN CONJUNCTION WITH
THE TRANSPORT MUSEUM, WYTHALL

PUBLISHING

888 ·
22
Kee

First published 2008

ISBN 978 0 7110 3316 0

© Malcolm Keeley 2008

Published by Ian Allan Publishing
an imprint of Ian Allan Publishing Ltd, Hersham,
Surrey, KT12 4RG

Printed in England by Ian Allan Publishing Ltd,
Hersham, Surrey, KT12 4RG

Code: 0810/B3

Visit the Ian Allan Publishing website at
www.ianallanpublishing.com

Front cover, main picture: Typical
working days for platform staff linked
towns with suburbs. S17 5717 and S23
5962 demonstrate at Solihull station
on 23 June 1973. *Malcolm Keeley*

Front cover, lower left: Midland Red
worked many intensive urban services,
such as the former tramway route from
Birmingham to Smethwick and Dudley.
D7 4544 leaves Birmingham on
29 June 1968. *Malcolm Keeley*

Front cover, lower middle: The
company is more fondly remembered
for its rural services. On 6 June 1965
S8 3268 encounters cattle between
Stafford and Newport. *Malcolm Keeley*

Front cover, lower right: Route 409
left Hereford at 0815 on Tuesdays,
Thursdays and Saturdays, returning
from Birmingham at 1825. On summer
Sundays a bus worked the opposite way
— perfect for 'townies' going fishing.
*R. Mallabon / The Transport Museum,
Wythall*

Back cover, upper: Loading in Paradise
Street, Birmingham, in the late 1950s
is 1949 GD6-class Guy 3560 on the
arduous 140 route to Dudley.
The Transport Museum, Wythall

Back cover, lower: Midland Red's last
new buses were Leyland National 2s.
No 823, delivered in 1980, bears
Tamworth's 'Mercian' local identity.
Malcolm Keeley

Right: Staff at Banbury in the 1920s.
The Transport Museum, Wythall

Contents

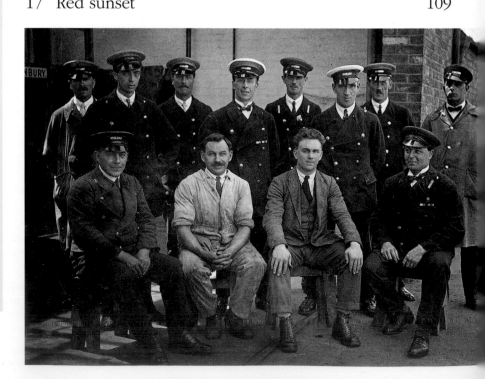

Introduction

I SHOULD WRITE A BOOK.

How many people have you heard say that, or the equivalent 'You should write it down or your memories will be lost'? Andrew Gardner, editor of the Transport Museum, Wythall members' magazine *Omnibus*, thankfully badgered several people to do just that. Just in time, because sadly those who remember the old company are passing on. So when the publishers asked for a book on what it was like working for Midland Red, there was a store of valuable memories to raid for you.

Thirty years ago, three of us wrote a two-volume history of Midland Red, published by the Transport Publishing Company. The story has been re-told since, usually concentrating on the vehicle development, with perhaps some reference to the garages. This book assumes that the reader has a basic knowledge of the company from these earlier books as we go exploring new angles. I am pleased still to have at my side Paul Gray to assist me in this mission, plus a host of other helpers, including the third of the co-authors, John Seale. Particular thanks are due to Phil Crook, Peter Jaques, Stan Letts, Dick Nutt, Paul Roberts and Roger Torode for their substantial assistance. Roger kindly marshalled the splendid advertising literature in this book and, in turn, thanks Mike Rooum for his considerable input. Paul Addenbrooke, Andrew Gardner, Phil Ireland, John Rollings and Dave Taylor have also been very helpful.

The characters of the prewar partners in running the company, Chief Engineer Loftus George Wyndham Shire and Traffic Manager Orlando Cecil Power, come over clearly from people's stories. Surprisingly, as it is nearer our own time, the postwar General Manager, Donald Sinclair, is much harder to know. When *Classic Bus* magazine nationally conducted a readers' poll for the greatest busman of all time, Donald Sinclair headed the list. There was a late plea that the quite exceptional engineering skills of Mr Shire place him ahead of Mr Sinclair. People like Shire ruled by terror, even by prewar standards. I am quite convinced that Mr Sinclair showed better man management skills to soundly direct the whole of his multi-faceted organisation, as well as showing the industry the way on vehicle design.

These top managers remain well known, but it is pleasant to recall those further down the tree. For example, both William Semmons and Dick Nutt praised the genius of Arthur Parkes who, as a 'back room' personality, would be astonished and probably unimpressed to be remembered in the 21st century. Amusing to note that the Engine Shop men admired by Dick Nutt are the same people despised

Above: The centre of power — Bearwood offices. This is the 1923 extension with the curved display windows that must have been fearsomely expensive at the time. The windows lasted for decades with little damage — a more civilised age. *The Transport Museum, Wythall*

as 'Bearwood Fumblers' by one of Bob Mills' driving colleagues at Dudley.

I never worked for Midland Red, but a portion of the company was sold to the West Midlands Passenger Transport Executive, my employers, in 1973. I became familiar with BMMO customs and made many new friends. Later my immediate boss was Paul Addenbrooke, who had joined Midland Red in 1951 as a general trainee. Over three years he spent time in every office and section, except the General Manager's office and the typing pool. The legacy of the war between Messrs Shire and Power cast a long shadow, and Paul became familiar with the then strange structure of the company, even after a major reorganisation undertaken under Mr Sinclair.

Paul noted that there were no Divisional Managers (they came much later); each department had its own Divisional Superintendents, and, rather than an overall Garage Manager, each garage had a Traffic Superintendent and an Engineering Superintendent reporting to their respective Divisional Superintendents. The divisional allocation of garages was quite different for each of the departments. Lines of communication could be quite convoluted, especially if there was any clash of personality at any level; no one person was in charge.

Above: Look out, the bosses are about! Directors and senior managers of Midland Red pose alongside the coach used for many years for directors' visits. This was FHA 425 (postwar fleet number 2293), one of 25 ONC coaches built in 1939. It was designated LON (Luxury ON) in its days as the directors' coach and had a different rear axle. *BMMO*

Above right: Smile please, or do the best you can. A coach party alights from a BMMO C1 around 1950. *The Transport Museum, Wythall*

Below: Leamington conductor Ashley Wakelin relieves a young lady of her fare on board a D9 in 1975. Ashley became associated with Wheels of Nuneaton and subsequently acquired the right to use the 'Midland Red Coaches' name. *Patrick Kingston*

When Paul joined in 1951, there were nine Divisional Traffic Superintendents, five Divisional Engineers and six Disciplinary Officers (as the Staff Dept officers were designated). In addition there were two driving schools and four conductor schools. This all led to a garage organisation with multiple reporting lines and no consistent pattern for the identification of performance on the road.

The Divisional Staff Officers (designated Disciplinary Officers) and the Training Schools handled staff management functions in totality for platform personnel. This meant that the Garage Traffic Superintendents had no direct impact on those who worked for them, or what penalties were handed out for misdemeanours.

Midland Red had an excellent magazine called the *Staff Bulletin*, not to be confused with 'Staff Notices' that told the troops what they should and should not do. Staff magazines tend to obsess over sport. The editor for decades, W. H. Pine, covered sport but, happily, included many inspired articles about past and current developments of the company, such as those by Raymond Tuft, Divisional Traffic Superintendent based at Leicester. You also read about the Midland 'Red' Symphony Orchestra, the Midland 'Red' Male Voice Choir and the annual show of the Horticultural Society with the monster honorary exhibit from Evesham garage, sitting in the fertile Vale.

It was a fascinating company and I am pleased to have had so much raw material from which to distil a flavour of what it was really like behind the glamour of those advanced-looking buses.

Malcolm Keeley
Shirley, Solihull, March 2008

The SOS – engine of expansion | 1

The British Electric Traction Company Ltd (BET) was formed in 1896 to develop electric traction throughout the country, and was soon a major player in the industry. Amongst many enterprises it purchased was, in 1899, the horse bus business of the Birmingham General Omnibus Co Ltd, which had gone into liquidation. BET operated the business directly for some years using the trading name Birmingham General Omnibus Department. Orlando Cecil Power was installed as Secretary, later becoming Traffic Manager. The entity used in 1905 to amalgamate all BET's omnibus assets in the city was an acquired but, so far, non-trading enterprise, the Birmingham & Midland Motor Omnibus Company Ltd. BMMO had been registered on 26 November 1904, and was described at the time by *Commercial Motor* magazine as 'the first attempt at a regular public service of motor vehicles worthy of the name'.

Motor-bus breakdowns were frequent, and the police constantly ordered them off the road — the most common reason being excessive noise. All the surviving motor buses were taken out of service in October 1907 and horse buses restored in their place. BMMO reintroduced motor buses in 1912 under the supervision of Loftus George Wyndham Shire as Chief Engineer. For over 30 years, BMMO would have no General Manager — the Engineering and Traffic Departments being controlled independently by Messrs Shire and Power, two forceful personalities who, not surprisingly, clashed from time to time.

Mr Shire chose the Tilling-Stevens petrol-electric chassis, their absence of gears making driving easier for ex-horse bus drivers. All existing horse bus routes were quickly converted to motor buses. An agreement was reached in 1914 with Birmingham that involved sale of BMMO city routes and the earliest motor buses to the Corporation.

The Birmingham deal encouraged the development of services to, or within, towns outside Birmingham. The outbreak of World War 1 in 1914 was a major blow to many other companies that had buses, or at least their chassis, requisitioned by the War Office. The Tilling-Stevens petrol-electric system was not approved of initially, however, so BMMO kept its fleet intact. Thus BMMO was able to

step in when both associated and rival companies had to withdraw facilities.

Postwar expansion

The War ended in November 1918 and there followed a time of intense competition. Many men had been released from military service with experience of driving and maintaining motor vehicles, surplus examples at reasonable price being within reach of the ordinary man for once in his lifetime as he received his war gratuity. Many truck, bus and coach operators began around this time. It is widely painted that an established operator like BMMO had to fend off these fiendish pirates. BMMO, of course, had only begun its outward march from Birmingham at the outset of the War, so one should have as much sympathy for the small man endeavouring to make a living in a totally deregulated environment.

BMMO set about consolidating its wartime gains and expanding into new areas, buying existing properties or building new ones to garage its buses. It had the advantage of size and the financial backing of the BET group. Development and dynamic promotion of services occurred wherever a reasonable return could be obtained. Sometimes BMMO would despatch a few buses to a selected district, with the necessary staff to man them, and

Right: In 1906 the infant BMMO received nine buses built by Brush, registered O 1283-91. This is Kyotts Lake Road depot, Birmingham. *MRK collection*

Above: The Tilling-Stevens 'Petrol-Electric' was powered by a four-cylinder petrol engine which drove a large dynamo. This provided electric power to a smaller motor which drove the rear wheels. There were no gears, making Tillings ideal in an era when motor vehicle driving was a new occupation. However a normal gearbox was much more effective, and later Tillings were suitably converted in the mid-1920s. Pieces of the solid tyres would go missing, so the conductor was treated to the sight of passengers at the rear jumping and nodding at each other as the blank bit hit the road. The single searchlight headlamp was a 48W bulb but was unable to search or light before the battery gave up in protest.

Like many companies at the time, BMMO often employed people who were related to existing good-quality staff. One such family is represented by the conductor of this well-laden 1913 Tilling-Stevens TTA2, O 9923, at the Stag & Three Horse Shoes. He is Mr F. E. Simper, but he was severed from the rest of the family, being transferred under the 1914 agreement to Birmingham Corporation Tramways. The driver was Mr W. Dixon, who completed 50 years' service with BMMO and its predecessors. *MRK collection*

a network of routes built up with the minimum of facilities. Competition would be challenged and, where practicable, eliminated. Following the successful agreement with Birmingham in 1914, arrangements defining areas of operation were agreed with Walsall Corporation in 1919 and Wolverhampton and Coventry in 1920. Not that BMMO moved into everywhere it fancied. BMMO eyed-up Northampton, and 1925 correspondence shows that several properties were under investigation. The local authority, however, was unhelpful in granting licences to ply for hire and the town remained peripheral to BMMO.

Although Leicester was to become one of the company's largest and most prosperous areas of operation, it was not until 1922 that a garage was opened there. A favourite story tells of 22-stone BMMO Inspector Bentley who, upon spying an 'opposition' driver near a wall, 'accidentally' leant upon the unfortunate with his arm across the poor chap's wind-pipe until the next Midland Red was loaded and away! It is doubtful that Mr Power intended the opposition to be crushed so literally. The same heavyweight is reported to have rocked violently a small 'opposition' bus full of passengers from side to side because the driver had annoyed him!

The company's campaign in Leicester highlighted that the competition was often armed with small, fast, light-weight buses that ran proverbial rings around the Midland Red Tilling-Stevens petrol-electrics. Mr Shire was conscious of this shortcoming. Initial thoughts to meet the threat involved, in 1921/2, the purchases of two small British-built Fords with 11-seat charabanc bodies and Garfords

Below left: The Worcestershire Motor Transport Company Ltd was formed in August 1914 to combine and develop the omnibus interests formerly associated with the BET tramways at Worcester and Kidderminster but only two months later had the majority of its vehicles requisitioned by the War Office. Arrangements were made for the services to be maintained by BMMO, and, as a result, Midland Red vehicles began to work from garages at Kidderminster and Worcester. Tilling-Stevens TS3 buses continued to be delivered until 1916. OA 7080-9 of 1915 had the usual forward-entrance Tilling bodywork, but OA 7090-9 received the 29-seat rear-entrance Brush & Birch bodies that had originally been mounted on the Worcestershire Motor Transport Leyland chassis taken by the War Department. OA 7093, 7096 and 7081 are seen at Kidderminster, converted to run on ordinary coal gas during World War 1. The gas bags were filled from roadside hydrants provided by the gas companies, and the arrangements were considered reasonably reliable. This is a later style of gas bag, with rigid sides, much better at coping with windy days. The central figure of the three in dark uniform is Mr E. F. Hickey, who later became Chief Disciplinary Officer.

It was a great relief to drive behind a glass windscreen but, as wipers had not been evolved, part of the driver's permanent equipment was a piece of apple or potato which, when rubbed on the windscreen, helped considerably in the rain. *BMMO*

Above: The supply of complete new Tilling-Stevens TS3 buses resumed in 1919, supplemented in 1920 by surplus War Department TS3 lorries, eminently suitable for bus or charabanc bodies. Services were opened up throughout the Midlands to link villages with towns. Staff posted leaflets through letterboxes, advising that Midland Red buses would start the next day. This would prompt disgust among the proprietors of horse-drawn carrier-carts that had long enjoyed villagers' patronage on market days.

Drivers and conductors in those pioneering days were paired together and kept the same bus. The driver of 1919 Tilling-Stevens OE 1133, William Webb (extreme left), was based primarily at Banbury but helped open up services at Wolverhampton and Tamworth. On Sunday mornings the driver, in unpaid time, had to examine his bus, for example removing the wheels and setting up the brake shoes. Mr Webb had survived some of the most famous engagements of World War 1 while serving in the Army's Mechanical Transport section. His engineering and driving expertise was ideal for the infant Midland Red when he joined upon demob in 1920. Also a private-hire driver, becoming a very well-known personality in Banbury, he retired in 1960.
The Transport Museum, Wythall

imported from the USA, with charabanc and bus bodies of various dimensions. These gave the company useful experience with lightweight vehicles.

Midland Red also tried to increase economic competitiveness by fitting double-deck bodies to Tilling-Stevens TS3 chassis converted to half-cab forward-control. A total of 56 double-deckers were built on earlier or new chassis between 1922 and 1924; the bodies featured an unusual layout for the time of front-entrance and staircase.

Mr Shire concluded that the company required a lightweight, reliable, straightforward design, as represented by the Fords, with the capacity of a full size single-decker displaying the Garford's nimbleness. The manufacturers

could not provide such machines, so Mr Shire decided that BMMO should build its own. BMMO was fortunately in the middle of an area where manufacturing industry was geared to the needs of the motor industry, and he was already sourcing items from the numerous engineering workshops. Wyndham Shire did not see any justification for installing arrays of machine tools or specialist manufacturing plants when such work could be done by firms expert in such activities.

The largest Garford, HA 2331, was fitted with a prototype engine designed by the company. Shire completed his first bus, registered HA 2330, in 1923. The company's products became known by the letters SOS, generally being called 'Soss' or 'Sosses' by those familiar with them. The initials are thought to mean 'Superior Omnibus Specification', but many think it was more along the lines of 'Shire's Own Special'. Shire would tell enquirers to make their own interpretation. This vagueness is typical of him and extended to the vehicle type names that followed. Engineering staff concluded that SOS stood for 'Sod Old Shire'!

The first model was known as the 'Standard SOS', only later becoming known as the SOS S, and was a very important step in the design of the British bus, changing the fortunes of the companies that operated them. It actually looked very similar to the preceding Tillings, and seating capacity remained 32. The bodywork was of lightweight timber construction. Outer panels were plywood, the only metal panels being those on each rear corner. The unladen weight was just 3 tons 13cwt, one of the principal clues to the improved performance over the previous Tillings. The 'Standard', however, featured a more reliable SOS gearbox, with four forward gears plus reverse, and plate-clutch transmission. The SOS four-cylinder petrol engine had a capacity of 4.332 litres. It was based on the Tilling design, but with Ricardo alloy cylinder heads and alloy pistons

Right: Bus services soon stretched well away from the company's Birmingham heartland. Tilling-Stevens OE 6187 of 1920 is seen in Melton Mowbray. Chassis were recorded in a series of Private Identification Numbers, first allocated in February 1923 but applied retrospectively to chassis disposed of between 1915 and 1922. Essentially they were allocated in order of delivery, each number being prefixed by the letter 'A,' and thus became known as 'A' numbers. These were not carried on the vehicles, being an internal paper exercise to keep track of the chassis. Their significance in Midland Red history came in 1944, when the A numbers replaced bonnet numbers as the fleet numbers carried on the vehicles. *The Transport Museum, Wythall*

Left: Puzzle vehicle. Tilling-Stevens OB 1111 was delivered with a bus body in 1916 but here carries a charabanc body, built probably by Tillotson in 1919. Swapping of bodies and even registrations was commonplace at this time. *The Transport Museum, Wythall*

giving a high-revving performance with plenty of power. The compression ratio of 5.6:1 was unusually high for the period, almost up to contemporary sports car standards.

Twenty-two 'Standard SOS' models were built in 1923. The first three chassis, HA 2330/3/48, were built entirely by BMMO, but the remainder were on Tilling-Stevens frames. Most were buses, but a minority were turned out as 32-seat charabancs. The 1924 production of 62 chassis was also based on Tilling-Stevens frames. Midland Red built five charabanc and 34 bus versions for itself, but the good performance of the 'Standard SOS' was attracting attention from sister companies in the BET empire which bought the remaining 23, beginning a considerable trade over the next 10 years. The buses supplied to these sister companies carried bodies to Midland Red specification.

Left: OE 7304 was one of the ex-War Department Tilling-Stevens chassis. Several entered service in 1920, with a selection of charabanc bodies; this one was ex-Scottish Motor Traction. It ran until 1926. *MRK collection*

The Birmingham & Midland Motor Omnibus Co., Limited.

MIDLAND "RED" MOTOR SERVICES

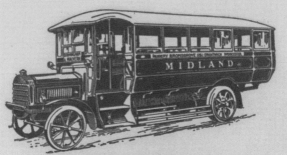

TELEGRAPHIC ADDRESS :
"OMNIBUS, BIRMINGHAM."

TELEPHONE:
2577 MIDLAND
BRANCH EXCHANGE.

CHIEF OFFICES:
547, BEARWOOD ROAD,
SMETHWICK.

PLEASE REPLY
TO
THE TRAFFIC MANAGER.

OCP/LEL.

OFFICES AND GARAGES :—

BIRMINGHAM	... 11, Bull Ring ... ... Tel. No. 886 Central.	KIDDERMINSTER ... 10, Vicar Street ...Tel. No. 108 Kidderminster
"	... 76, Lionel St. (Parcels) " 6513 "	LEAMINGTON ... Old Warwick Road " 194 Leamington
"	... 22, St. Mary St. (Stables) " 2769 Midland.	NUNEATON ... Coton Road ... " 213 Nuneaton.
EDGBASTON	... Waterworks Road ... " 967 Edgbaston.	SHREWSBURY ... Ditherington ... " 455 Shrewsbury.
BANBURY,	... Canal Street ... ... " 123 Banbury.	STAFFORD ... Newport Road ... " 230 Stafford.
BROMSGROVE	The Strand ... ... 125 Bromsgrove.	TAMWORTH ... Two Gates ... ... " 90 Tamworth.
		WOLVERHAMPTON, Bilston Street ... " 1366 Wolverhampton
		WORCESTER ... East Street ... ... " 485 Worcester.
		" " ... The Cross ... ... " 360 "

...ILL BE AVAILABLE ON
...CEPTED.

ALL QUOTATIONS BASED ON
NEAREST ROUTE
UNLESS OTHERWISE STATED.

September 28th 1922
CORPORATION TRAMWAYS.
RECEIVED
M. Inst. T.

Left: The upper saloon of the Tilling-Stevens double-deckers was still open to the elements, quite normal at this period. The upper-deck seats were arranged longitudinally; this 'knifeboard' arrangement, with the passengers sitting back to back, permitted a 'hump' in the lower-saloon roof to provide headroom for the gangway. Seating capacity was 29 downstairs and 22 on top. Bearwood, Leicester and Worcester received permanent allocations of these double-deckers, although other garages would borrow them and in time gained them in small numbers on their allocations. This is Malvern Wells terminus, a popular destination at holiday times. *The Transport Museum, Wythall*

Right: The Garfords' arrival coincided with the change to registering vehicles in Smethwick and beginning the long association with the 'HA' registration series. They were often employed to compete with other proprietors. The Fords and Garfords were used by the company for around three years before sale. *BMMO*

Above: Tilling-Stevens OA 343 on Gibbet Hill, between Coventry and Kenilworth. These ancient glass positives of the 1920s were hand-coloured for Midland Red and must have created quite an impression in an era when movies were still silent and monochrome. *The Transport Museum, Wythall*

Above right: This exceptionally interesting picture, taken at Malvern, features HA 2333, one of the two prototype Standard SOS buses with chassis built by BMMO, unlike many of the early Standards, which had chassis frames from Tilling-Stevens. The driver, Jack Hartland, felt unable to continue driving buses following a fatal accident that was not his fault, involving a passenger stepping off a Birmingham tramcar in the middle of the highway. He later resumed his driving career, but not in the bus industry. *A. R. Hartland*

Above: Overall dimensions of the Standard SOS were half an inch short of 25ft in length, 6ft 10in width and 9ft 7in height. General styling was based on the 1920 design, with the distinctive 'porch' entrance, pronounced rocker panels, and drop windows in all six main bays. The radiators looked similar to the Tilling design but were taller and narrower. Pneumatic tyres were standard but, unusually, the wheels were spoked. This one is seen at Ledbury. The Standard SOS heightened the performance inadequacies of the Tilling-Stevens TS3 buses, and in 1925/6 later Tillings in the Midland Red and Trent fleets were fitted with SOS gearboxes in lieu of their original electric transmission. *The Transport Museum, Wythall*

Production of Standard SOS models increased to 209 in 1925, of which 115 were intended for the Midland Red fleet and 94 for sister companies. Two of these sister companies are worthy of additional comment. Trent was BMMO's BET neighbour to the north, and good relations were assisted by the presence of Mr O. C. Power on the Trent Board of Directors from January 1923. Very satisfying, however, was the heavy investment by Northern General Transport. Its Chief Engineer was a young, talented ex-Army engineer, Major Gordon Hayter, whose views on how buses should evolve ran on similar lines to those of Mr Shire. Major Hayter had been experimenting with lighter, full-size buses by rebuilding earlier vehicles, but the SOS product met his requirements precisely. The Standard SOS truly redefined the British bus.

Although BMMO had deliberately refrained from competing with the BET-owned tramways in the Black

Right: Writing in the *Staff Bulletin*, the legendary Raymond Tuft, Divisional Superintendent for the Leicester Area, recalled starting a new Midland Red service in 1920s Nuneaton, advertising the new facility by hanging yellow handbills in the buses. He recalled scrutinising other proprietors' vehicles when he saw one with yellow bills pasted on the windows. The operator concerned was also starting the same new service with exactly the same timings. Close examination revealed that the bills had been taken from Midland Red buses, with the company heading and Traffic Manager's name cut off the top and bottom! SOS Standard HA 2377 is seen *en route* to Leicester. *The Transport Museum, Wythall*

Above: Buses would also be used on long-distance services, of which the first, commencing during 1921, in the solid-tyre era, ran to Weston-super-Mare and Llandudno. Luggage was carried in a large tarpaulin-covered wicker basket mounted on the roof, but these services could be so popular at holiday times that the fleets of buses were accompanied by a van carrying the luggage. This Tilling-Stevens van, loading in the Bull Ring, Birmingham, had previously been a bus. Midland Red maintained (or, later, hired) a fleet of motor vans to deliver goods throughout the area, this business being taken over by Pickfords in May 1934. The name 'Midland Red Parcels Express' was, however, retained, and parcels continued to be carried on Midland Red buses. These parcels could be collected from and delivered to authorised agencies on the company's network of routes. *The Transport Museum, Wythall*

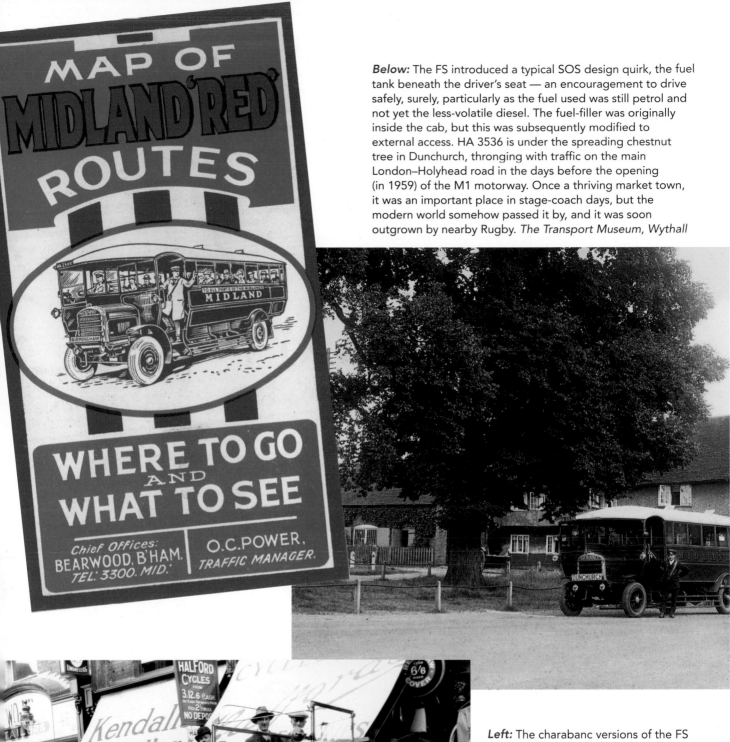

MAP OF
MIDLAND 'RED'
ROUTES

MIDLAND

TO ALL PARTS OF THE MIDLANDS
MIDLAND

WHERE TO GO
AND
WHAT TO SEE

Chief Offices:
BEARWOOD, B'HAM.
TEL. 3300. MID.

O.C. POWER,
TRAFFIC MANAGER.

Below: The FS introduced a typical SOS design quirk, the fuel tank beneath the driver's seat — an encouragement to drive safely, surely, particularly as the fuel used was still petrol and not yet the less-volatile diesel. The fuel-filler was originally inside the cab, but this was subsequently modified to external access. HA 3536 is under the spreading chestnut tree in Dunchurch, thronging with traffic on the main London–Holyhead road in the days before the opening (in 1959) of the M1 motorway. Once a thriving market town, it was an important place in stage-coach days, but the modern world somehow passed it by, and it was soon outgrown by nearby Rugby. *The Transport Museum, Wythall*

Left: The charabanc versions of the FS — represented here by HA 3526, undertaking an outing for Birmingham Education Department — were delightful-looking machines. However, the driver was separated from his passengers, and in 1929, after only three years, all 18 were rebodied as single-deck buses. The 'new' bodies were actually extensively rebuilt lower decks from forward-entrance Tilling-Stevens double-deckers, all of which had been withdrawn by this time. *T. J. Edgington collection*

Country, this permitted other operators to abstract the traffic and, from 1924, the company was asked to operate over the tramway routes to give the opposition a run for its money. From 1926 onwards, Shire's SOS buses began to replace the various tramways as well as open up new routes, creating a network and requiring more garages. New operating agreements with the local authorities in Dudley and West Bromwich were signed in 1929 and 1930 respectively. Away from the Black Country, Midland Red buses replaced the Burton & Ashby Light Railway in February 1926 and the Kidderminster to Stourport tramway in November 1928. In 1926 BMMO's fleet of nearly 600 vehicles covered more than 16 million miles and carried more than 60 million passengers.

One further bus had been built in 1925. This was HA 2500 — the first SOS to be built with driver alongside the engine. This released more space in the passenger saloon, permitting an increase in seats to 34. Nearly all the bus and charabanc vehicles for Midland Red in 1926 were of this new design known as the FS, meaning 'Forward Steering'. Each year would see new models, often employing parts non-interchangeable with those of the previous year, when it might have been more helpful to await a comprehensive redesign. Restorers at Wythall of SOS buses of this vintage have concluded that Mr Shire got completely drunk every New Year's Eve, burnt all the plans and started afresh the next day as so few parts seem to fit from one year's production to the next! There is no evidence for this fiendish allegation, by the way!

The year 1928 would be the record year for SOS production. The programme included no less than 349 buses and 30 coaches, of which around half were for the Midland Red fleet. Thus began the story of the SOS. Its reputation and that of Mr Shire was now assured, but he continued to

Above: The 1927 production mostly comprised a further new model, the Q (for Queen). The front bulkhead of the body was moved as far forward as possible, the engine protruding slightly into the passenger saloon and covered by a plate. This allowed the seating capacity to be increased to 37 in a vehicle that weighed only 4 tons 4cwt 2qr. The cab was considerably shorter, and in partial compensation the engine, bonnet and radiator were all offset by varying degrees towards the nearside, although the cab remained fearsomely cramped. HA 3684 and friends load in Coventry before the opening in October 1931 of Pool Meadow bus station. *The Transport Museum, Wythall*

Below: The Q design was modified by a reduction in height to become QL ('Queen Low'). This was achieved mainly by employing smaller, disc wheels, with twin wheels replacing the large singles at the rear. Another important improvement was the adoption of four-wheel braking, earlier vehicles having brakes on the rear wheels only. A significant way of identifying a QL from a Q lay in the main body panels, which were deeper on the QL, while the rocker panels below were shallower, on account of the lower chassis frame. *The Transport Museum, Wythall*

evolve one new design after another with an increasing emphasis on passenger comfort. Performance also improved as six-cylinder-engined vehicles occupied an increasing proportion of new vehicles. Mr Shire was enormously respected throughout the industry and it is a wonder that he was not headhunted by a major manufacturer. Perhaps he turned the offers down, or his difficult personality meant such approaches never came his way.

Below: There were charabanc versions, known as the QC and QLC, that shared family features with the contemporary Q and QL buses but differed in one most important respect by reverting to normal control (with the driver behind the engine). This returned the driver to the passenger saloon for the company's first proper touring coaches, designed to work the new programme of extended tours. The then popular term 'charabanc' (the literal translation from the French being 'wagon with benches') was an appropriate description for those vehicles in which passengers filed through separate doors to each row of seats. On these coaches, however, long-distance passengers for the first time entered by one entrance, at the front, gaining access to the comfortable seats via a central gangway. This gangway, of course, cost seats, and the coaches accommodated only 30 (later 29), albeit in considerable comfort. It is curious today to recall that short-distance bus riders enjoyed the benefit of a roof but that long-distance coach passengers travelled in the open, unless the hood was raised. These coaches retained the roll-type hood, but permanent glass side windows, in polished frames, and a fixed rear dome were great improvements, which meant that the driver could slide the hood into place much more easily from the central gangway than hitherto — an important point in the event of a sudden shower. This is a QC model. *The Transport Museum, Wythall*

Left: SOS QLC HA 5138 touring on Dartmoor. *The Transport Museum, Wythall*

2 | Orlando Cecil Power faces regulation

Mr O. Cecil Power JP, M Inst T.

Whilst Mr Shire's SOS buses were a major factor in the successful growth of Midland Red and some of its sister BET companies, the commercial wisdom of the other major player in the management of the company, Traffic Manager Orlando Cecil Power, was just as important.

The enormous influx of new buses around 1928 was not only a reflection of ongoing replacement of Tilling-Stevens TS3 buses, but also important service developments, especially in Worcester. The Corporation had the right to purchase the city's tramways, operated by the BET-owned Worcester Electric Traction Co Ltd, 28 years after 1 May 1901. Using powers obtained in 1926, the Corporation acquired the tramways with a view to converting them to trolleybus or motor-bus operation, and running buses on many roads outside the city. Ignoring the advice of the General Manager of Birmingham Corporation Tramways, acting as consultant, to convert to trolleybuses with supplementary motor-bus services, an agreement was entered into whereby BMMO would operate all the city services on behalf of the Corporation. Midland Red buses took over from the trams on 1 June 1928. The successful agreement formed the basis of most other subsequent agreements between the company and local authorities.

The 'big four' railway companies had gained powers to operate bus services in 1928 and this really had caused the big bus groups, like BET, to break into a sweat. Until then, they had been able to crush much of the competition, but suddenly here were potential rivals with similar financial muscle. Fortunately the railway companies decided on a different route by approaching major bus companies and buying into them, thus sparing a wasteful fight. On 24 April 1930 the Great Western Railway and the London, Midland & Scottish Railway purchased half the ordinary shares of BMMO, and became represented on its Board of Directors. The Great Western Railway, a pioneer bus operator in its own right, possessed a few local services and these were merged into Midland Red services by 1932.

A few days after the railway investment BMMO purchased, on 30 April 1930, Black & White Motorways Ltd of Cheltenham, one of the principal operators of long distance coach services. Black & White retained its separate identity, however, and its control was shared with two other companies, Bristol Tramways and City of Oxford Motor Services.

Prior to 1930 omnibus licences were issued only by local authorities which cared to adopt the necessary powers, and thus in many places no licence of any kind was required. Consequently, BMMO did not normally purchase established businesses. It was simpler to start up a competing service, rather than spend money on a purchase, with no guarantee that there would not be further opposition from yet another operator the next day. The Road Traffic Act 1930 brought regulation to the industry through Area Traffic Commissioners who, before granting 'road service licences', considered representations by persons already providing transport facilities along or near a proposed route. Operators obtaining such licences thus enjoyed the protection of the Traffic Commissioners. Gone were the days when independents could poach on the company's best routes, and similarly, Midland Red could no longer use its superior might to crush the opposition. Between 1931 and 1939, more than 150 small businesses would be purchased by BMMO to consolidate the company's network.

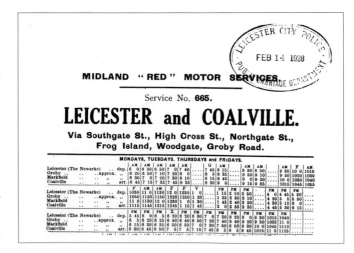

The arrival of the Road Traffic Act 1930 must have cramped Mr Power's style, even though there were clear benefits of protection within it. As the company had grown, Mr Power may have become remote from those on the ground. Moreover, those employees had changed too. The carnage of World War 1 was a clear demonstration that those in charge, one's betters, did not necessarily know what they were doing, and that authority should be open to challenge. Those returning from military service were promised a land fit for heroes, but instead they got continuing poverty that, in 1929, turned into serious economic depression. Other countries had seen revolution but the nearest Great Britain got to serious anarchy was the 1926 General Strike.

Two memoranda speak volumes about Mr Power's attitude to the Road Traffic Act, which was effective from 1 April 1931, and his astonishment that he could no longer assume the loyalty of all his staff. An interesting by-product of the division of responsibilities between Shire and Power was that drivers were regarded as quasi-engineers under the aegis of Mr Shire and conductors were under Mr Power, each with quite different uniforms of brown and blue respectively. The memos included the odd slight to Shire's drivers who had to handle primitive vehicles, sometimes overloaded, especially on Saturdays and Bank Holidays. It also indicates how relatively small buses replaced tramways in the Black Country — it was evidently achieved by overloading (although the term then meant any degree of standing).

The first memo, dated 20 June 1931, was addressed to all inspectors and copied to all traffic officials:

CLAUSE 19. ROAD TRAFFIC ACT
If you are not aware of the fact, Clause 19 of the Road Traffic Act deals with drivers' hours, limiting their working time to a maximum of 8.5 hours in one shift, or two shifts of 5.5 hours with a break in between.

The conductors are also being put on the same scale with a view to keeping working arrangements to a certain extent in unison.

A regulation has just been issued by the Minister of Transport with regard to overloading, limiting the number of standing passengers to five. You have already been circulated on this matter, and the latest instruction is that you will carry on with the overloading to the same extent as has previously been in operation. The probability is that we shall have to obey the Law at a later date, but meanwhile I want you to explain to the conductors what the effect will be if we carry the regulations out rigidly. Briefly these are as follows:

(1) It will mean that we shall have to put more 'buses out at peak hours which will increase the number of awkward shifts and split turns; in other words we shall have to turn 'buses out for about one hour in the morning and two hours in the evening which will naturally mean increasing the Staff of drivers and conductors. This will automatically re-act on the men who are already employed, inasmuch as the extra men taken on will have to take their share of the work

that is going, and it will mean still further reducing the number of hours that will be available.

(2) It will also mean that we shall have to increase the number of vehicles, particularly on Saturdays which will necessitate a further increase in the number of men employed and an automatic reduction in the working hours available.

I want you to convey to the men in a quiet manner the text of this letter so that they will understand the position as it stands.

As previously stated, I have given instructions for the overloading to continue, and I want each and every man

Above: The type designation of the new-generation rear-entrance double-deckers was self-explanatory, being originally DD and changed to DD(RE) in 1934 after the introduction of forward-entrance double-deckers. The DD(RE)s, better known in later life as REDDs incorporated the RR2LB 6.373-litre petrol engine and a new heavier-duty gearbox, introduced in 1931 and known as the 'Silent third' because of its quietness (compared to its predecessors) in third ratio.

Mr Shire was delighted when his production batch of 50 REDD double-deckers, bodied by no fewer than four builders, began to arrive in 1932. The mood was short-lived, for he was livid to discover that they were a fraction too high for all but one of the doorways at Bearwood garage. The bodybuilders were not at fault, which didn't help at all. Shire went into overdrive, involving almost everyone in the design of a suitable height warning system. Soon, when a REDD approached any of the offending doorways, a series of flashing lights and klaxons would burst into life to warn the driver. Unfortunately many drivers would consider it a point of no return, ignore the warnings and scrape through, providing that they were certain the boss was not on the premises! This might explain why the REDDs migrated to Leicester, where Metro-Cammell-bodied HA 8044 still looks fine in postwar years. It now carries the Private Identification 'A' number as its fleet number — 1412. *R. Marshall to understand that in the event of him being prosecuted for overloading, I am prepared to defend the case and foot the bill. Also explain to the conductors that their licences will not be jeopardised in any way.*

If you find any men who absolutely put their backs up and refuse to carry more than five in excess of the seating capacity, I want reports in each and every case.

Representations are being made to the Minister at once by The Omnibus Owners' Association and others, asking for a deputation to be received to explain the difficulties experienced by Operators in regard to overloading on certain occasions, and we hope to get the Order rescinded or considerably modified.

I want it understood that I do not approve of ridiculously heavy overloading, so do not go from one extreme to the other.

Explanations obviously did not go well, as can be seen by the second memorandum, dated 19 August 1931. The importance then of earning sufficient income in the summer for the company to financially survive the winter will be clear. Readers need to know that, in those days, the August bank holiday was on the first, rather than last, Monday of the month.

GENERAL
I am astounded to find many things have happened during the last week or two which indicate that we have got quite a number of men, Drivers and Conductors, and an occasional Inspector here and there, who are working definitely and deliberately against the Company's interests, and incidentally in the long run, their own.

I am referring first of all to certain men refusing to carry more than 5 passengers even on August Saturday and Bank Holiday Monday; and even last Saturday and to-day there are men refusing to help us to put some money on one side to pay our and their wages during the winter.

It is reported that in a number of cases Drivers have interfered in regard to the loading of 'buses. As you know, this is no concern of theirs, as the Conductor is responsible for the loading, and I cannot understand why Conductors allow their Drivers to interfere, and also why Inspectors don't let Drivers know quite straight that they MUST not interfere.

Secondly, I understand that certain men, Drivers particularly, are insisting on working the Road Traffic Act to the letter, and when they are standing by refusing to run as a double on a local service etc.

Well, as you are aware, if they are going to adopt that attitude we shall have to do the same, and as I intend having all the 'buses at work whenever they are required, we shall have to engage extra men to take over these 'buses when they are standing by, as THE WHEELS MUST TURN.

Thirdly, we are having a large number of complaints of 'buses rushing by waiting passengers, incivility, discourtesy,

Midland "RED"

AND

RAILWAYS JOINT MOTOR SERVICES

MAP OF BLACK COUNTRY DISTRICT

Left: The double-deckers may have created excitement, but production of single-deckers continued too. HA 6235 was a 1931 IM6 type, one of an increasing number of saloons built with six-cylinder SOS petrol engines. Seen in Birmingham with postwar fleet number 1305, it ran until 1951. *G. H. Stone*

etc; in fact it makes me feel that the 'OLD MIDLAND 'RED' PRESTIGE' has gone, frittered away by an ungrateful lot of men who ought to be ashamed of themselves.

I can scarcely believe that our men could behave in the way they are doing, especially in view of the recent concession in regard to the Union Agreement re: payment of overtime twice over. I am very, very disappointed, and can only assume that you, and our supervisory staff, and our outside officers, have lost touch with the men, as I am sure in the old days we should never have put up with such ingratitude. My only answer is, that if the men will not play the game, then they shall have the Road Traffic Act in every detail, which will hurt them more than it will hurt the Company.

I still think, however, that reason will prevail, and I want you to get every outside official to put the case before the men in a sensible, reasonable way, and see if we can stop the rot. We have only got a few weeks to earn our money, and it is rotten if the men won't help while we are busy.

Mr Power, incidentally, was sympathetic to the Transport & General Workers' Union, actively campaigning for members in the company. Mr Power preferred to deal *'with people who represent the whole of the men and not a portion of them. I should really be much more satisfied if at no distant date, the Union are able to say that they represent 100% of the Company's employees.'*

There was, of course, one way to accommodate more passengers without increasing the number of crews. This was to re-introduce double-deckers, and Mr Shire had a rear-entrance prototype, HA 7329, ready in 1931. Double-deckers would form an increasing part of the fleet from now on, and the first production batch of 50 was constructed in 1932.

On 1 July 1934 a major step was taken towards a co-ordinated nationwide coach network, in which partners pooled specified services and operated them as an indivisible whole, eliminating wasteful competition. This was 'Associated Motorways', in which BMMO was an important partner.

BMMO first participated in a joint service with a municipality in 1935, namely West Bromwich Corporation. Joint services were subsequently arranged with the transport departments of the Corporations of Birmingham, Walsall and Leicester.

Important purchases, effective from the end of June 1935, were two subsidiaries of the Balfour Beatty Group. One was Stratford-upon-Avon Blue Motors Ltd, operating under the fleetname Stratford Blue, with whom Midland Red had agreed a working arrangement in September 1932. This delightful company was surprisingly retained as a subsidiary for many years. Even more extraordinary, Midland Red's subsidiary standardised initially on second-hand Tilling-Stevens vehicles and, from 1948, on new Leylands. The other was the Leamington & Warwick Transport Company, which had by now replaced its trams with buses. A considerable number of new single-deckers were allocated to Leamington where, on 1 October 1937, Midland Red buses took over from the subsidiary company.

Bus stopping places were evidently another problem for Mr Power around this time. A memorandum dated 9 January 1936 entitled 'Regulations re 'Buses Stopping for Passengers' includes the following comments:

'I think we must all admit that on thick town services, we shall have to adopt "Fixed" and "By Request" stopping places, as owing to the extra traffic on the roads, it is difficult at busy times for the men to keep time, owing to the number of stops. I do not, however, want men to get into the habit of not stopping when hailed even between agreed stops.

'I am satisfied that if we have "Fixed" and "By Request" stopping places, a great majority of the passengers will collect at these stopping places and the emergency stops in between would be reduced to a minimum. I shall be glad if you will go through the various town routes in your district and let me have your suggestions as early as possible, as to where "Fixed" and "By Request" stopping notices should be placed.'

P. 200r, 10-29.

The British Electrical Federation, Limited.
Form AT/27 — 24-9-26

MEMORANDUM.

Name of Company | .... B. & M.M.O. ....

To .... Miss. Mann. .... April 15th, 19 31.

From ...... Traffic Manager. .... Our Ref. ARC/BLN.

Subject ...... SALARY. .... Your Ref. ....

Will you please note that your salary has been increased at the rate of 2/- per week as from week ended April 10th.

O.C.P.

Left: Miss Doris Mann may have been left reeling at her heady increase of two shillings (10p) per week in 1931. She joined Midland Red straight from commercial school and dedicated her working life to the company. From 1941 she was in charge of the Central Waybill Office at Bearwood, responsible for the smooth working of the waybill organisation throughout the system and the final checking and analysis of these very important conductors' documents. She was also the Honorary Secretary of the Central Committee for the company's 'Twenty-Five' clubs, for long-service employees.

Right: Enormous passenger demand on Bank Holidays meant anything that could move was on the road. This saw buses borrowed from fellow BET subsidiary Potteries loitering in Birmingham between journeys on its X1 service to Hanley. GVT 112, a 1939 Weymann-bodied Daimler COG5, and, on this occasion, its own crew are seen in Station Street, Birmingham, ready to run 'on hire' to Dudley, where the Zoo was a major attraction. *R. T. Wilson / The Transport Museum, Wythall*

Sending out an SOS | 3

Mr Shire continued to develop SOS designs right through the 1930s. After a plethora of designs, things became more settled after the last four-cylinder buses, single-deckers delivered in 1933/4.

The new standard single-decker was the ON (Onward). This took almost full advantage of the maximum length for two-axle single-deckers of 27ft 6in, which, combined with the compact SOS petrol engine, allowed 38 seats. The 1934 production included ON buses for sister companies — the last deliveries to other operators except Trent, which continued to receive SOS chassis until 1940.

Naturally Mr Shire was interested in the economical diesel-engined vehicles then appearing throughout the country. Three buses were built with AEC A171 7.7-litre indirect injection diesel engines and classified DON (Diesel ON). The AEC engine was 6in longer, however, which meant an appropriate reduction in the passenger saloon, reducing the capacity to 36 seats. The next contract of single-deckers for the Midland Red fleet was for 100 vehicles, split between ON petrol and AEC 7.7-powered DON diesel buses, delivered from late 1934 into 1935. Diesel engines by several manufacturers were experimentally fitted into some ON and DON buses as the company developed its own unit.

Midland Red put its own diesel engine, of 8-litres capacity and called the K-type, into production in 1936. Its design was so compact that, unlike the AEC unit, it did not affect the bonnet length. Forty-four ON buses were converted to diesel with these units in 1937/8, and re-classified CON (Converted ON). Following an earlier, petrol, prototype with Cotal epicyclic gearbox, the first production batch of 65 SON (Saloon Onward) buses with SOS diesel engines and orthodox gearboxes was delivered in 1936. More batches of SON buses would be built up until the outbreak of World War 2 in 1939.

On the double-deck front, after experience with the 1932 rear-entrance double-deckers, which became known as the REDD type, the company's predilection for front entrances surfaced again from 1933 with the prototype of a design to become familiarly known as the FEDD. Early FEDDs had six-cylinder petrol engines but, after the 1936 deliveries, later FEDDs had the 8-litre diesel units.

The coach fleet was considerably modernised in 1935. By now, forward-control service coaches had developed into the LRR (Low Rolls-Royce). Modernisation of the touring coach fleet came with a new type, the 29-seat OLR (Open Low Rolls-Royce). Like a few other high-quality tour operators, Midland Red evidently considered a bonneted

Right: Radiused window corners were by now standard, but the front end of the ON family additionally received gentle curves and large radiused corners to the windscreen itself. The front of the roof featured a slight hump, as if a destination-blind box was intended, but, sadly, the bulkhead stencils and destination boards remained standard, notwithstanding the use of roller blinds on contemporary double-deckers. The driver continued to sit on the fuel tank, and the cab door was still only partially glazed. This was Midland Red's first diesel bus, 1934 DON HA 9481, with AEC 7.7-litre engine, seen postwar at Leicester working the 665 to Coalville, its home garage. In 1951 it became the Leicester-area tree-lopper.
MRK collection

Right: Delivered in 1934 but seen postwar, HA 9431 was one of the first production batch of 50 front-entrance double-deckers (FEDD), with bodies by Short Bros. Petrol engines were standard, but this bus had the distinction of being fitted from new with the first SOS diesel engine. *MRK collection*

Left: Batches of FEDDs were delivered throughout the remainder of the decade, the 1935/6 deliveries having all-metal Metro-Cammell bodies. These were the last with petrol engines. The excellent quality of the bodies meant that it was worthwhile converting them to diesel between 1942 and 1947, employing AEC 7.7-litre or BMMO K-type units. A good load awaits departure from Station Street, Birmingham. The rather upright front permitted a row of four seats together, ahead of the staircase above the cab; this both increased the capacity to 56 seats and introduced a much sought-after location for families! *G. H. Stone*

Left: The 50 SLR-class coaches of 1937 were handsomely rounded machines, although arguably their lines were spoiled by the then fashionable stepped waistrail, necessitated by the seats' being at different levels to improve the vision of passengers in the back rows. English Electric supplied the 30-seat coachwork. Major refurbishment after World War 2 included replacement of the SOS RR2LB petrol engines with Leyland E181 7.4-litre diesels, as well as the fitting new grilles and simplified mouldings. They were also reupholstered throughout, in the process losing the green — a colour Mr Sinclair hated! This is CHA 994 after refurbishment. *The Transport Museum, Wythall*

Right: English Electric also bodied some SON buses. DHA 637-736 of 1937 included styling features from the SLRs, notably full-drop windows, with pillars that were thicker at the top. SOS vehicles of 1937 and early 1938 had the fuel tank on the offside of the chassis frame, thus allowing a conventional cab door. This was the height of the streamline era, and when new these SONs were painted in a flamboyant variation of the standard livery. Many DHAs worked from Leamington, but 732 was more familiar at Digbeth and then Kidderminster. Any reference to SOS on the fronts of vehicles was removed after Mr Sinclair took over, but they continued to be called 'Sosses' by those who knew them. *The Transport Museum, Wythall*

Left: More SONs were delivered in 1938/9, bodied by English Electric and, later, Brush. They had orthodox livery and window pillars and reverted to the earlier layout, with the fuel tank under the driver's seat. This is Worcester Street, Birmingham, after World War 2, with the blitz-damaged Market Hall providing the backdrop. EHA 742 awaits departure on the 198 via Curdworth to Tamworth, its home from 1954 to 1956. *G. H. Stone*

vehicle with driver in the passenger saloon and opening canvas roof was still the best specification for a touring coach, but actually this style of vehicle was on its way out. Low build was considered important on both types, which employed petrol engines.

Two more batches of coaches were built before the outbreak of World War 2 in 1939. These were the 50-strong SLR (Saloon Low Rolls-Royce) class of 1937 and the 25 ONC (Onward Coach) class of 1939. Both types had full width cabs to streamline their appearance. The SLRs had petrol engines but the ONCs were diesel-powered.

Mr Shire also put four quite exceptional vehicles on the road in 1936-7, becoming familiarly known by their registration numbers, BHA 1 and CHA 1-3. Although their REC classification stood for Rear-Engined Coach, actually only CHA 1 was a coach, the other three being service buses. Carlyle Works constructed all four bodies. They were technically extraordinarily advanced for the UK. They had the driver sitting ahead of the front axle with, on the buses, the entrance alongside. The SOS petrol engines were positioned transversely at the rear of the frame, behind the rear axle.

Work on the first REC chassis began in 1934, hence its Private Identification A number (1591) among that year's deliveries. It seems that the chassis performed well on its lengthy road trials, the inevitable teething problems being successfully cured. Trouble only arose when BHA 1 took to the road as a bodied vehicle. Only top-link drivers were allocated to it and all of them declared the bus impossible to drive. The usual BMMO constant-mesh gearbox was mounted towards the rear and connected by a series of rods to the gear lever in the cab. The quiet SOS petrol engine was now so far away as to be silent, thus rendering almost impossible the established art of double-de-clutch gear changing, required before synchromesh. The first official photographs of BHA 1 were taken in May 1935, but it was not licensed until February 1936, being mothballed until the French-built Cotal electromagnetically operated epicyclic gearbox, then being tested in an ON chassis, could be fitted into it to provide two-pedal control. Beans Industries of Tipton, already a supplier to Midland Red, apparently began manufacturing Cotal gearboxes under licence and three were purchased for CHA 1-3.

Above: Further FEDDs delivered in 1938/9 had composite-construction Brush bodies of different appearance, with manual jack-knife doors in recessed entrances. This is EHA 294, seen on Hagley Road West near the King's Head, Bearwood, with postwar fleet number 2162. This 1938 batch had fuel tanks on the offside of the chassis frame. *G. H. Stone*

Above: The last Black Country tramway conversion involved the routes from central Birmingham along the Dudley Road to Bearwood, Soho and through Oldbury to Dudley. It required further operating agreements with the local authorities of Smethwick, Oldbury, Rowley Regis and Tipton. It went ahead on 30 September 1939, despite the outbreak of World War 2 earlier that month.

The group of services were given local Birmingham service numbers B80-89 and theoretically were operated jointly with Birmingham City Transport. Basically, however, BCT ran the B80-83 to Bearwood, Soho and short workings, whilst Midland Red ran the B84-89 beyond to Smethwick, Oldbury and Dudley, although there were exceptions to balance the mileage between BCT and BMMO, creating appealing photographic targets for enthusiasts. Most of the final batch of FEDDs, FHA 836-85, was allocated to garages providing the replacing bus services. Along with the last SONs, these FEDDs had more rounded bodies. *MRK collection*

Above: The 1939 ONC vehicles, with 30-seat Duple coachwork, introduced the simple but extremely effective livery of red below the waistrail and black above that became standard for coaches, including the SLRs, after World War 2. FHA 420 displays postwar fleet number 2288 at Carlyle Works, in the company of one of 23 Morris Commercial trucks bought between 1947 and 1950. *The Transport Museum, Wythall*

Below: ONC interior. *The Transport Museum, Wythall*

4 | William Semmons CBE

Mr William James Semmons, CBE, celebrated his birthday on Sunday 24 July 2005. Then 101 years old, there was something special that he wanted to do the next day: he wanted to see the five resident SOS buses at The Transport Museum, Wythall, just south of Birmingham. It was exactly 73 years to the day that he joined BMMO at Bearwood. **Paul Gray** was privileged to meet him.

William Semmons' career had begun at the vehicle manufacturer Thornycroft as a fitter. He began in the repair shop but the foreman had recognised his potential and arranged his transfer to the Experimental Department.

He joined BMMO as an engineer in the Experimental Department. His first role was to read all of the relevant technical journals and précis articles of relevance for L. G. Reid, the Chief Assistant Engineer. William didn't think much of this job, as he wanted to build and develop some of the new ideas he was reading about. Upon making his wishes known to Shire and Reid, he received both sanction and encouragement — and the new title of Experimental Engineer. Reid, incidentally, was quite different from Shire, normally calm, mild-mannered and easy to work with. William's brief was to assist with the development and building of a new direct-injection diesel engine. His work also took him to see other SOS users, including Northern General where he got to know Major Hayter, the company's Chief Engineer and his assistant, Donald Sinclair, who would later become General Manager at Midland Red.

William recalled that everyone in the engineering section seemed to live and breathe Midland Red, some claiming that their dreams and nightmares were no different. It was also quickly apparent that Shire was an exceptionally talented engineer who was highly respected, almost revered, by those around him. His standards were such that everything had to be perfect — good was not acceptable. Those unable to make the grade and the unfortunates who turned out poor work were dismissed. Shire unfailingly acknowledged a good job, however, and he was always supportive when genuine design and manufacturing difficulties were encountered.

William considered that the most valuable member of the engineering team at Bearwood was Arthur Parkes. He had started as a fitter and went on to develop outstanding skills. He could 'make anything', working from a drawing

Above: The revolutionary BHA 1 of 1935, with Mr Shire studying the installation of the SOS BRR-type six-cylinder petrol engine at the rear. *The Transport Museum, Wythall*

or simply following a conversation with Shire or others. He could even prepare quite complex patterns for castings.

Everyone in the engineering team had to be a proficient bus driver, and the afternoon arrived when William was summoned. As a motor-car driver he wasn't too worried by the command 'Take a bus out and don't come back until you can drive it', until Shire bundled him into the cab of a double-decker. A more formal drive, under the watchful eye of the Chief Instructor, followed.

An annual difficulty was fog. In the early 1930s vehicle lighting was not particularly effective and the fog caused many accidents. Each winter, Shire would fit a number of Bearwood's indigenous fleet with fog lamps from almost every manufacturer. The engineers, including William, were cajoled by Shire to take out the buses on foggy evenings and report their findings. It was unpaid overtime, of course, and by way of a sweetener, Shire encouraged the engineers to take their wives or girlfriends with them! William and his wife had many a foggy ride round in anything from a splendid new ON to a tired Q or QL.

Unfortunately, working on the Shire team included a less pleasing task, that of 'spy'. Whenever possible, he was to travel to and from his home on Hagley Road West by Midland Red bus, incognito, of course, and not using his travel pass. Any fault on the bus had to be noted, the number and garage being recorded and the appropriate authority advised.

Back at Bearwood, despite the Engineering and Traffic Departments being rather distant entities, all aspects of the company seemed to function like clockwork. Shire always met Power's demands for the correct number and type of buses at any given garage, sometimes with little notice.

Mr Semmons' work on the new diesel engine concerned many facets of the design, in particular its combustion chamber. All engine testing was done in-house, the Experimental Department having first call on the sole dynamometer owned by the 'Red'. Not surprisingly, Shire took a keen interest in all developments relating to buses, be it concerned with bodywork, chassis, or running units, to lighting, paint finishes and upholstery. Part of William's remit was to visit trade shows, always under an assumed name. In a rare display of humour, when William received his pass to an agricultural trade show he found that Shire had registered him in the name 'Farmer W. Hayseed'.

Once the new SOS diesel engine was running successfully, and with further prototypes in build, there was a desire to compare it with others. In 1934 Shire instructed Semmons to assess the different engines available. William recommended that three types — an AEC 7.7, a Leyland 8.6 and a Gardner 5LW (the 6LW being too big) — be purchased for fitting into ON chassis. To the pleasure of Shire and all those involved, the fuel economy of the SOS prototype proved better than that of the AEC and the Leyland. The Gardner was impressive in this respect but not in others, and it was AEC that secured the orders until the SOS unit entered production.

The 'industrial espionage' worked both ways. William and his colleagues were amused by how often representatives from bus chassis and engine builders would 'ride the Red'. This was probably most prevalent after the introduction of the ON model and again when the diesel-powered examples took to the road. Sometimes the visitors introduced themselves to the bus crew, others rode anonymously. When BHA 1 was released, the VIP visitor levels rose to a new high.

A good, close working relationship soon blossomed with AEC, Mr Semmons no doubt becoming known to AEC engineers in the course of designing the installation of the A171 7.7-litre engines in the DON buses. The expertise William had built up meant he could comment on this engine and was no doubt effective in expressing his ideas. AEC's regular man at Bearwood was George Robinson who, in turn, became familiar with the SOS diesel engine. Robinson suggested to AEC's Chief Engineer, John Rackham, that the pair of them sample the engine in service. This would have meant that Mr Semmons spent the day with Rackham who was impressed by the SOS diesel unit, and evidently by William too.

William left Midland Red at the end of 1936 to join AEC as a man with new ideas, obtaining high-level backing to plunge into at least two costly experiments immediately. He developed the toroidal form of direct-injection used on most AEC engines from 1938, including units in AECs and wartime Daimlers delivered to Midland Red. William would not remain at AEC for very long for towards the end of 1940 he was seconded to the Department of Tank Design at Woodlea, Virginia Water.

It was with sadness that the museum learned of the death of Mr Semmons peacefully in his sleep on 29 June 2006, just a few weeks away from his 102nd birthday. His depth of knowledge and ability to recall events of so many years ago were an inspiration. With his humour and the ever-present twinkle in his eye, he will be remembered with affection.

We asked William to sum up Mr Shire. He answered without hesitation: 'a very clever man with a strong personality and much admired. You would die for him — or swing for him. That was how he was.'

5 | Promoting between the World Wars

O. C. Power's early career included being on the staff of the United States Consulate in Birmingham under a former editor of the *New York World*. The gentleman wanted to turn OCP into an American newspaperman but this was not to be. Nevertheless Mr Power was a firm believer in the value of newspapers and his background must account for the flair of the advertising produced by Midland Red.

Below: Early premises in Sutton Coldfield.
The Transport Museum, Wythall

MIDLAND "RED" MOTOR SERVICES

SALOON BUSES AND MOTOR COACHES FOR PRIVATE PARTIES AT CHEAP RATES

MIDLAND "RED" ENQUIRY OFFICE

REGULAR AND RELIABLE SERVICES TO:—
CANNOCK, ECCLESHALL, LICHFIELD, MILFORD, NEWPORT, PENKRIDGE, RUGELEY, SANDON & WOLVERHAMPTON. FREQUENT LOCAL SERVICES TO COMMON STATION, DOXEY, LITTLEWORTH, LOTUS WORKS, RISING BROOK, STONE ROAD AND WEEPING CROSS &C.
CONNECTIONS TO ALL PARTS OF THE MIDLANDS

BOOKING & ENQUIRY OFFICE

MIDLAND RED MOTOR SERVICES
DISCOUNT TICKETS SOLD HERE

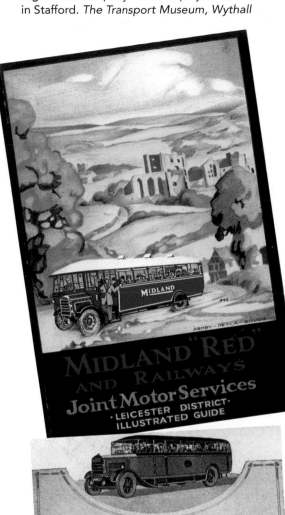

MIDLAND "RED" AND RAILWAYS
Joint Motor Services
·LEICESTER DISTRICT·
ILLUSTRATED GUIDE

WILLS'S
MIDLAND RED
TOBACCO
PER 10½d. OZ.
STRAIGHT CUT VIRGINIA

Have Your Holiday!
THE
Midland "Red" Way

Anywhere Tickets will cost you Five Shillings a day

CHIEF OFFICES:
BEARWOOD,
BIRMINGHAM
Tel. Bearwood 2020

O. C. POWER,
Traffic Manager

299·48
MILES
299 MILES HAVE BEEN COVERED IN ONE DAY BY A PASSENGER USING A 5/- ONE DAY ANYWHERE TICKET

MIDLAND "RED"
CIRCULAR TOURS
WORCESTER
BY
ORDINARY SERVICE 'BUSES.
WORCESTER DISTRICT

Below: With its multitude of red and white enamelled signs, the enquiry office in the Bull Ring, Birmingham, was undoubtedly eye-catching. From 1930 these premises were also home to the growing Long-Distance Services Department, transferred from Bearwood. The Bull Ring building had to be given up in 1937, so the company moved to a former gentlemen's clothing emporium in nearby Worcester Street. *The Transport Museum, Wythall*

See the Country around BY
MIDLAND "RED"
Frequent Services from Great Malvern

Circular Tour round the Hills, Upton-on-Severn, Tewkesbury, Evesham, Broadway, Worcester, Whitchurch, Ross, Droitwich, Ledbury, Upton Bishop, Birmingham, etc., with convenient connections TO ALL PARTS OF THE MIDLANDS.

PRIVATE HIRE.

Have your Outings by Midland "RED" Cosy Coaches. Illustrated Booklet of Midland "RED" Tours may be had on application to all Offices and Agencies.

Local Booking & Enquiry Agent:
FERRIS' TRAVEL BUREAU.
3 Promenade, Gt. Malvern.
Tel. 343 Gt. Malvern.

4/6. ANYWHERE TICKETS. 4/6.

Available Tuesdays, Wednesdays, Thursdays and Fridays, and can be obtained at all Offices and Agencies. Travel on any Ordinary Service Bus, and Change Vehicles or Routes as often as desired.

Chief Offices:
BEARWOOD,
Birmingham,
Tel. 2020 Bearwood.
O. C. POWER,
Traffic Manager.

MIDLAND "RED" MOTOR SERVICES.

ROUTE GUIDE SERVICE No. 133

Birmingham to Coventry

2665

HAS anyone ever threatened to "send you to Coventry?"

If so, you realise that, for some reason or other, you have merited their displeasure, and that you are to be punished therefor.

Next time anyone uses the threat to me I shall certainly reply that, if the journey is to be made by a "Midland Red," I shall be prepared to take my punishment like a man.

6 | DMS takes over

Right: The LRR service coaches and OLR touring vehicles were relegated to bus work during World War 2. The OLRs were extensively rebuilt from normal to forward-control to permit a more effective 34-seat capacity, an increase of five. AHA 632, recently arrived from Evesham on the 148 service, waits opposite the hub of the company's parcel-distribution network in Dudley Street, Birmingham.
G. H. Stone

Left: Warwick (Emscote) garage was closed as services were cut upon the outbreak of World War 2 but reopened as Leamington came under enormous pressure following the Coventry blitz. All 31 members of the LRR class eventually gathered at Leamington, these high-geared downgraded coaches being ideal for the open roads between Coventry and nearby towns.
R. A. Mills / The Transport Museum, Wythall

Right: Bengry of Leominster, trading as Primrose Motor Services, was one of many operators hiring vehicles to Midland Red in the 1940s. Seen at Hereford (with hire board visible behind the windscreen), Strachans-bodied Leyland Lion PLSC CVJ 481 was previously owned by Western National and registered VW 202. *R. A. Mills / The Transport Museum, Wythall*

The outbreak of World War 2 in 1939 meant the production of buses, including the company's own vehicles, had to stop. Fuel rationing caused suspension of around 200 services, and reduced frequencies on 700 others. There was a complete halt to long-distance coach services. Loads increased considerably, however, with factories at full stretch for the war effort, people leaving blitzed cities for the comparative safety of the countryside, and petrol rationing for private cars. Auxiliary conductors were used in the peaks; these were volunteers travelling free and supervising loading while the conductors collected fares under crush-load conditions. Other operators' vehicles were hired with drivers, Midland Red providing conductors. The War also brought, for the first time, lady bus drivers. Interior and exterior lights were masked, making buses less visible to enemy aircraft, but life hard for night drivers and conductors. A number of vehicles were commandeered, whilst parts of certain garages were requisitioned for the war effort.

Evacuation

Several thousand children had been evacuated to Rugby, which was then itself declared a vulnerable area. Midland Red agreed to move them in two days' time. 50 buses were sourced from Tamworth, Coalville, Leamington, Nuneaton, Hinckley, Leicester and Rugby plus 16 from United Counties into whose territory the children were destined. Raymond Tuft got all the individual instructions ready, plus a summary.

Operations were to begin at 9am and the ex-military Traffic Inspector had the buses lined up immaculately in three rows. The Rugby Billeting Officer greeted Mr Tuft with the comment: 'I'm so glad you've come. Look at all these buses — what are we going to do with them?' Mr Tuft told him to sit on the fence and watch. The exercise was child's play to Midland Red, as each driver was given his own detailed instructions and ticked off on the summary. The biggest evacuation job of the War went off with military precision, leaving the Billeting Officer

amazed. Midland Red would undertake many more evacuations during the war.

Those were one-offs but, after the big air raid of 14 November 1940 devastating Coventry, there were massive moves to nearby towns every evening, returning to Coventry the next morning. The Kenilworth and Leamington routes were particularly affected. Buses and coaches of all descriptions were pressed into service, and staff brought to Leamington garage from far afield.

The Ministry of Supply eventually permitted the limited production of buses. The completely SOS fleet was joined in 1942 by nine Leyland Titan TD7 and six AEC Regent double-deckers. Fifty-eight Gardner 5LW-engined Guy Arabs and 33 Daimlers with pre-selective gearboxes and AEC 7.7 engines, all double-deckers, arrived by 1945, the year the war ended.

Mr Shire retired in 1940 and the man who replaced him, Donald McIntyre Sinclair, was quite different. The quietly spoken Scotsman had served an engineering apprenticeship of five years with Albion Motors in Glasgow. He moved up via several posts in the transport industry to become, in 1931, Assistant Chief Engineer of Northern General Transport, the well-known BET operator in the northeast of England. NGT had favoured SOS machines for many years so their capabilities were well known to Mr Sinclair. NGT was equally innovative and had produced side-engine single-deckers to maximise seating capacity. Mr Sinclair would add style to Mr Shire's splendid but generally conservative-looking workhorses.

Mr Shire deserves the credit for combining the concept of removing the engine from within the body space to increase the seating with that of placing the entrance and the driver ahead of the front wheels. However, the rear engines had only been a moderate success. Drastic design changes to BHA 1 were planned but World War 2 intervened. Shire's active and innovative mind devised placing the engine on its side and positioning it amidships under the floor but his thoughts got no further than sketches before retirement. Mr Sinclair's Northern General years had also convinced him that the underfloor engine, mounted amidships, was the future. Experimental Engineer Jack Ransome developed Mr Shire's plans to eventual success. A K-type diesel engine was laid over to within five degrees of the horizontal (allowing a fall for the oil to drain away from the cylinders), repositioning the injection pump to the front and fitting a new sump. The final arrangement proved brilliant in its simplicity and required the minimum of new design work. Adapting the existing engine resulted in the crankshaft centre line falling nicely in line with the gearbox and rear-axle drives with cylinder heads and injectors, the air cleaner and the injection pump being wholly accessible from a comfortable sitting position on the offside. Also, because the engine was positioned just behind the front wheels, the pipes connecting the engine cooling system to the massive front radiator were relatively short and, given a powerful water pump, cooling was perfectly adequate.

Extensive bench-testing followed the engine modifications and, when the latter proved successful, BHA 1 was subjected to drastic surgery to become the prototype test vehicle. All four prewar rear-engined vehicles were extensively rebuilt as underfloor-engined single-deckers. The bodies were swapped in the process, including the sale of the coach body of CHA 1, and an entirely new body built for CHA 3. The quartet was joined in 1946 by a fifth, entirely new, prototype, HHA 222. This introduced chassisless construction and was bodied by Metro-Cammell, which had experience of the concept with prewar trolleybuses for London Transport. A new type of code system was evolved, the five prototypes being styled S1-5.

In October 1943 the Traffic Manager, Mr Power, died suddenly, and shortly afterwards Mr Sinclair was appointed the company's first General Manager. He additionally retained the role of Chief Engineer until relinquishing the

Above: Nine Leyland TD7 Titans and six AEC Regents joined the fleet in 1942. Six of the Leylands had Duple bodies to severe austerity design. The other three, however, had well-rounded bodies by Northern Counties, a builder permitted to continue using metal frames. This is 2440; by luck another of the trio is passing in the opposite direction. *The Transport Museum, Wythall*

Left: Several Guy Arab buses followed. Six delivered in 1942 had Weymann austerity bodies. Two more, 2499 and 2500, arrived in 1943 with interesting bodies intended for Manchester Corporation and bearing that operator's distinctive design features. They had Metro-Cammell metal frames finished by Weymann as 56-seaters. No 2500 ran for nearly all its life from Sutton Coldfield garage and is seen in High Street, Birmingham. *R. A. Mills / The Transport Museum, Wythall*

title to Mr S. C. Vince in January 1946. Mr Sinclair prepared for a return to normal manufacture. The SOS name was dropped and replaced by the company's initials, BMMO.

Mr Sinclair did not anticipate, at this stage, moving the engine on double-deckers. However he decided to modernise their appearance dramatically by concealing the radiator, using a grille design that had a family connection with the single-deck fleet. The first experiment in 1942 used a prewar FEDD, but an entirely new prototype double-decker entered service in 1945, registered HHA 1 and becoming type-coded D1. The new bus reverted to a rear entrance and the sleek body, built by Weymann, featured only four window bays on the lower deck, like the London RT, and had much improved destination blind arrangements. The chassis closely followed the specification for the immediate prewar FEDD, with K-type 8-litre engine. In 1949 it received platform doors prior to their adoption on all new BMMO double-deckers.

Right: All 33 wartime Daimlers had austerity bodies and were allocated to Digbeth, Birmingham, but later became familiar at the city's Sheepcote Street garage after the latter's opening in 1951. Brush-bodied 2549 loads at the Red Lion, Earlswood, terminus of the 179 to Birmingham via Tidbury Green. *G. H. Stone*

Below: The remaining 50 wartime Guys were Arab II models, shared between Leicester (Sandacre Street) and Sutton Coldfield garages. The last five were received in 1945 and had bodies by Northern Counties, still allowed metal frames and curved window corners, softening the appearance considerably. No 2587 loads for Barkby at Leicester's St Margaret's bus station, opened in June 1942. The concrete shelters looked indestructible but were spectacularly drab. *J. P. Addenbrooke*

Left: BHA 1 in its second incarnation, as an underfloor-engined bus with radical ideas on front-end design. This working day is going wrong — the conductor looks on as the driver peers underneath at Perry Barr, Birmingham, *c*1949. *Ron Herbert / The Transport Museum, Wythall*

Right: CHA 2 looks more like the postwar buses we would become familiar with but retains sloping pillars. As originally rebuilt it had opening vents on alternate windows and a single-line destination with number, subsequently being further rebuilt to the condition seen here. This is the patch in front of Digbeth garage, lost when the road was widened to create a dual-carriageway. *G. H. Stone*

Left: A group of the company's lady drivers pose with CHA 3 and its brand-new body in August 1944. *BMMO*

Right: Rear view of CHA 3, also on the patch at Digbeth, although this bus was not associated with that garage. *G. H. Stone*

POLICE REPORT
Thursday 11 October 1945

SUBJECT: Overloading of Public Service vehicle

Sir,

I have to report that at 4.05pm, this day, I went to Lea Bank, Bewdley Hill, Kidderminster, in the Police car. At 4.15pm, a Midland Red bus, single-decked, reg'd No EHA 768, Service No 291, came from the direction of Bewdley Hill down Lea Bank.

I signalled to the driver to stop, which he did, and I then noticed that the omnibus, which was a 38-seater, appeared to be carrying more than the permitted number of passengers.

I interviewed the conductor, Samuel George Sly, aged 58 years, and told him that I was going to count the number of passengers on the omnibus. He replied, 'All right, most of them are schoolchildren.'

Upon entering the bus I found it contained 68 schoolchildren, and 15 adults, total 83 persons. The majority of the children were seated four in a double seat and 16 were standing in the gangway. All the adults occupied a seat each.

Sly agreed to the count I had made and said, 'The Company have issued instructions that two children count for one adult, or four children occupy one double seat. At that rate I am not overloaded as I am also allowed to stand 12 adults at a peak period, or 24 children.'

I told him that the facts would be reported.

Left: FEDD 2167 (EHA 299), with the prototype full-width bonnet, concealing the radiator, fitted in October 1942. The front of the upper deck was restyled too, and the beginning of the postwar design is clear. *R. A. Mills / The Transport Museum, Wythall*

Right: The stunning 1945 D1 prototype, 2541, registered HHA 1 — giving rise to its nickname 'Harry One'. It was bodied to Midland Red's design by Weymann — possibly because partner company Metro-Cammell had not yet resumed bus production. Metal body frames would be standard for the postwar fleet. How modern this must have looked alongside the old 'Sosses' and the severe wartime buses. *BMMO*

Left: The first Metro-Cammell-bodied S6 buses to enter service were 3001 and 3006, in December 1946. Early S6s were built with the nearside of the driver's cab open above the waistrail to improve vision through the nearside windscreen in the dark. However, this led to fearsome draughts, so a sliding window was fitted.
The Transport Museum, Wythall

Above: S6 3024 in High Street, Leamington, in June 1960. There remained two separate crew rotas at the Leamington garages. One covered essentially the out-of-town services, the other the 'Track' routes (L41-5/50) developed from those absorbed from the Leamington & Warwick Transport Co; this latter, constituted by Act of Parliament, continued to exist as a registered company, and a further Act was required to dissolve it. Midland Red had to pay to its non-operating subsidiary company the net profits on each route, on the proportionate route-mileage basis pioneered at Worcester.
Patrick Kingston

Coping with peace

1946 saw the fleet strength at 1,426 buses, of which no fewer than 1,204 were repainted during the year, most as 'quickies' to lift the appearance of the run-down stock. Nearly 347 million passengers were carried in 1946, increasing to 374 million the next year as people yearned to get out and about after the years of war.

Vehicle production was reintroduced at Carlyle Works, but serious delays were encountered at the bodybuilders. BMMO was the first to adopt wholeheartedly the underfloor engine layout. One hundred S6 single-deckers, delivered in late 1946 and during 1947, represented the fruition of wartime development work. They started a new fleet number series from 3000 upwards. Despite the chassisless S5, for the time being BMMO reverted to separate body and chassis for ease and speed of production. The horizontal BMMO 8-litre engine was fitted with a BMMO-designed constant-mesh gearbox made by David Brown.

The S6 bodywork contract was divided between Brush and Metro-Cammell, setting the supplier pattern for the next few years. Detail differences between the two were discernible to the skilled eye. Forty seats were provided in the 27ft 6in body. The destination and route number roller blind layout, first seen on the D1 prototype, was adopted as standard. The number of standard bay lengths was reduced to six; the side window size would be used on all BMMO-built buses until 1966. Cab access was by a hinged door on the offside, another hinged door being provided at the saloon entrance. The front door arrangements on the S6 now look archaic, as power doors did not arrive until a few years later. Despite this, with its underfloor engine and entrance ahead of the front axle, the S6 is historically of immense importance as the trendsetter for single-deckers throughout the country. It took the other manufacturers four or five years to catch up with BMMO.

Midland Red took advantage of the newly permitted wider dimension of 8ft with 100 S8 buses. It is widely assumed that there was never an S7, the model number jumping to S8 because of the width. A further 300 similar vehicles appeared in the years 1949-51. These were intended as the S9 and S10 types but the last 44 single-deckers took advantage of revised vehicle dimensions and were classified S12. They were built to a length of 29ft 3in, permitting 44 seats. By 1953 all the earlier single-deckers from S6 onwards had been similarly extended and upseated.

Mr Sinclair had firmly settled upon underfloor-engine single-deckers, but he was determined to improve further the company's buses. He undertook a long tour of North America in 1948 and set up Bus Design Committees the following year. One result was almost certainly S9 No 3441, which did not enter service until March 1950. It had a redesigned front end by Carlyle Works from new and was known as the S9 Mk I. The new square front incorporated electrically operated platform doors, access to the cab being via the saloon rather than by a separate offside door, and the cab was not partitioned from the rest of the vehicle.

Some of the S10 production run included further experimentals. No 3703 was the solitary S11, being fitted with independent front-wheel suspension and re-designated S10 when conventional suspension was fitted in 1957. BMMO was developing a bigger engine of 10.5-litre capacity, and 3634 was fitted with a prototype unit at various times between 1952 and 1956.

No 3694 was the prototype S13, designed from new as a 30ft-long vehicle with a 17ft 6in wheelbase, compared to the 16ft of the S6-S12. It entered service on 1 June 1950; the first day buses of the new length were permitted. Three more prototype S13s appeared in 1951, 3877/9 with bodies built by Carlyle itself, the second of which was a 40-seater

Right: No 3292 demonstrates the extra width and modified windscreen of the S8 at Leicester Southgate Street. The garage yard was not only used for certain Midland Red, Barton and Lincolnshire Road Car bus services, all represented here, but was also the start point for services and excursions to London, Great Yarmouth, Skegness, Mablethorpe, Cleethorpes, among other destinations. An internal letter describing the congestion there recorded that on 1 August 1959, during a glorious summer, no fewer than 35 vehicles were despatched to Great Yarmouth on a single departure. *Milepost 92½*

Above and right: Some working days can go very badly indeed. Midland Red was proud to announce that the S8 was 'The Most Stable Bus in the World', achieving in excess of 41° on the tilt test (the legal requirement being 35°) thanks to the greater width and the location of the engine beneath the floor, but this didn't save 3229 when it ran off the road in June 1949 at Tintern, overturning several times down an embankment. The body was extensively damaged but demonstrated remarkable strength, and the bus returned to service in February 1950. *Metro-Cammell*

Below: The first C1, 3300, was the only one to have a recessed near-side screen, albeit not matching the offside. *MRK collection*

Right: The partition around the driver of the C1 was dispensed with on the C2s, intended for extended tours. The driver sitting with the passengers was seen as a desirable feature of this type of operation, as it had been when normal-control tour coaches had been reintroduced in 1927. From 1954 C4 coaches took over most coach cruises, but a few extended tours operated over roads requiring coaches of lesser dimensions, so C2s 3351/4/6 remained on coach-cruise work. In 1959 they were upseated from 26 to 30 and modernised with new grilles and bumpers, being joined in 1961 by 3345. This is 3356 at Carlyle Works after its facelift; the C2s had both windscreens recessed from new. *The Transport Museum, Wythall*

to dual-purpose specification, suitable for both ordinary stage carriage services and the longer 'X'-series routes. No 3878 was bodied by Willowbrook. The production S13s arrived in 1952/3 with 40-seat bodywork by either Brush or Nudd Bros & Lockyer — later Duple (Midland) — to 40-seat dual-purpose standard. The exception was Nudd-bodied 3919, with two doors.

The first 45 postwar coaches were built in 1948/9 with chassis based on the underfloor-engine service bus. The centre-entrance Duple 30-seat bodies to BMMO design were 7ft 6in wide, as 8ft-wide vehicles were initially confined to specially approved routes, not convenient for vehicles likely to be used for private hire. Their stylish appearance was very modern compared with contemporary designs. The driver sat in a half-height partitioned cab, accessed by an external door. Twelve similar C2-class coaches followed in 1950, with only 26 seats as they were intended primarily for extended tours. Access to the C2 cab was through the interior of the coach.

With BMMO capacity fully occupied building revolutionary single-deckers, the first 100 postwar double-deckers were based on AEC Regent II chassis with 7.7-litre AEC engines and crash gearboxes. Mr Sinclair modernised their appearance with concealed radiator bodies based on the D1 prototype, with four-bay all-metal construction. The vehicles took the classification AD2.

By the time Metro-Cammell was delivering its half of the AD2 contract, Brush was already bodying 100 further double-deckers, this time on BMMO D5 chassis. These were followed by a further 100, the D5B class, featuring another new innovation, electrically operated platform doors.

There were to have been eight Regent IIIs with air-operated pre-selective gearboxes and air brakes to form the AD3 class, but the order was cancelled. The D4 is something of a mystery. It is thought to have been a prototype 7ft 6in-wide BMMO double-decker, but surviving drawings show a width of 8ft, so the reasons for its abandonment are not known.

There were also 20 Guy Arab III double-deckers, classified GD6, delivered in 1949 that were totally non-standard in the fleet. They lacked the stylish postwar Midland Red design features although the exposed radiators, half-drop ventilators and rain deflectors were still normal elsewhere. Almost certainly they were accepted in standard manufacturer's form for quick delivery. The bodies were also built by Guy, based on metal-frame shells supplied by Park Royal. The vehicles had constant-mesh gearboxes and vacuum-servo brakes, but their principal point of interest was their engines. They were fitted with Meadows 6DC engines of 10.35-litre capacity, the largest in swept volume on the British bus market, but compact enough not to require the extended bonnet of the typical Gardner 6LW-powered Arab III.

The huge increase in travel demand during the early postwar years meant that pre-1934 petrol-engined buses had to carry on well beyond their intended lives. Most buses from 1934-45, with the notable exception of the excellent metal-framed Metro-Cammell-bodied FEDDs, had their bodies extensively rebuilt to extend their lives. This had to include relatively modern but deteriorating wartime bodies; the work at the same time softening their austerity lines.

All petrol vehicles were withdrawn from passenger service by the end of 1952, and the rebuild programme ended. Indeed, the supply of new vehicles was sufficient to allow the withdrawal of later single-deckers which had not received extensive rebuilding, including from the last delivery of 'prewar' saloons — some 1940-built SONs.

Left: Clearly demonstrating why 7ft 6in-wide coaches were favoured for certain Scottish cruises, 3309 inches past Scottish Motor Traction H56 (FS 5578) at St Mary's Loch, between Moffat and Selkirk. The Burlingham coach body of the SMT dates from 1949, the same year as the modern BMMO C1, but is based on a 1933 Leyland TS6 chassis. *J. P. Addenbrooke*

Right: Following the experimental equipping of D1 double-decker 2541 with power doors the concept was extended to single-deckers with S9 3441. As can be seen, the entire front end was redesigned, and the separate driver's door on the offside eliminated. The deep bumpers and polished-aluminium mouldings with raised fleetnames became a feature of the company's more radical prototypes around this time. No 3441 started life at Bearwood but was transferred to Leicester Sandacre Street in readiness for the new X97 service to Shrewsbury, which commenced on 7 October 1950. This picture is dated 5 August 1950.
T. W. Moore collection

Left: A company loudspeaker van toured the X97 route during the week before its introduction, an inspector broadcasting details of the service and distributing leaflets. They obviously did well, as duplicates were required on the first couple of days and on subsequent weekends. The van, FHA 699, was a 1939 Fordson 15cwt and is seen here at St Margaret's bus station, Leicester. *BMMO*

Right: The Brush body of the first 30-footer, S13 prototype 3694, repeated the brightwork used on 3441. It is seen outside its home garage, Cradley Heath. *S. E. Letts*

Left: In 1951 there began a programme to lengthen all early postwar single-deckers to 29ft 3in to permit upseating by four, to 44. Fortunately the long wheelbase, with the rear axle placed well back, facilitated the conversion. Metro-Cammell lengthened S10 3600 in 1951, but Roe carried out all the other rebuilds, handling the S8s in 1951/2, the S9s in 1952, the remaining S10s in 1952/3 and finally the S11 and the S6s in 1953. S6 3076 is nearest the camera in this view, recorded at Roe's works in Leeds. *J. P. Addenbrooke*

Right: Lengthened Brush-bodied S10 3615 at Nuneaton bus station demonstrates the finished result, identical to the S12s. Brush was by this time employing stainless sliding vents. More opening ventilators were provided on standard bodies from the D5 and S10 onwards; the Metro-Cammell AD2s (3150-99) were also bodied late enough to receive them. *Alan D. Broughall*

7 | Driving in the 1940s

Left: Between 1946 and 1949 Carlyle Works refurbished the bodies of around 50 ON-family single-deckers, the work varying from very thorough overhauls to extensive rebuilds of a rather severe style using metal frames. AHA 497, carrying postwar fleet number 1602, was one of the latter. *The Transport Museum, Wythall*

Below: Rebuilt to a similarly severe style by Samlesbury in 1948 were six 1934 Short-bodied FEDDs, including 1578 (HA 9443). Less obviously, Nudd Bros & Lockyer attended to a couple more in 1949, represented by 1565 (HA 9430) with sliding vents. This is Digbeth. *G. H. Stone*

R. A. (Bob) Mills worked for Midland Red during this interesting postwar period with several generations of buses running alongside each other. He worked at Dudley garage between 1946 and 1950, and then did another nine years at Digbeth. He became a driver during the dreadful winter of early 1947. His memories start there:

'There was another severe snowfall one night followed by a piercing north wind that rapidly caused drifts almost everywhere. I was marked up for the early Oakham turn, the D7 service which ran from Gornal via the Himley Road to Grace Mary Estate. The staff bus had some worrying moments with the numerous drifts but eventually I found myself preparing to set out with a BHA-registered FEDD; without a shovel. A message had been left by the Traffic Superintendent — would we try to get as far as the colliery?

'We struggled along Oakham Road as far as the Tansley Hill Road turn. Inexperience meant I drove around the corner without investigating and into that north wind. And the most extensive snowdrift I have ever encountered. There we stuck; attempts to reverse only made it worse, the rear end sliding into deep, fresh snow. I struggled back to a phone box to convey the sad news and was told to wait for assistance, whenever that may be. The wind was steadily piling snow ever higher and it was by then level with the destination blind. Around 11am a housewife appeared with tea — truly an angel of mercy.

'About 2pm they arrived, four of them, mixed drivers and garage staff, with two shovels. After around 90 minutes, shovelling around the wheels, each of us taking turns, we were rewarded with movement. All volunteers gave a helping push, and I was able to reverse about a quarter of a mile before a slightly less snowbound area allowed me to turn round. We then returned to the garage to join numerous buses that would normally have been out on service.

'Before the long-awaited thaw there came a final send-off. I had three trips on our notorious 140 [Birmingham–Blackheath–Dudley] service. Traffic delays meant we were an hour late leaving Birmingham on the second trip. In the traffic queue nearing the Kings Head, I was further dismayed to find that the bus, another BHA-registered FEDD, was sliding gently towards the gutter whenever we stopped. Falling temperature was causing the surface to freeze. Traffic was lighter past Warley Odeon and down the hill. Halfway up the other side was a BCT Daimler, 1321 — a South African Daimler COG6. It was at right angles across the carriageway, with rear end gradually sliding into the heaped snow along the gutters. The driver seemed unable to control the wheelspin, which was getting his rear wheels into deeper trouble by the second.

'No hope of getting past, so I parked well away, walked around to the platform and recruited half-a-dozen good-natured stalwart males. With some remaining BCT people we soon straightened 1321 out. I was strolling back to our trusty steed when this sweet young thing appeared, picking her way through the snow in elegant court shoes, much

Above: The first 50 AD2s (3100-49) were bodied by Brush and delivered in 1948. The remaining 50, 3150-99, were bodied by Metro-Cammell, which could not deliver them until 1949/50. The products of the two builders were easily distinguished. The Brush bodies had only four sliding ventilators on each deck. Early Met-Camm drawings looked identical, including a thick, shaped moulding where the upper and lower decks joined. In the event, eight vents were standard by the time the Metro-Cammells were delivered. Both decks were built together, thus not requiring the moulding between them.

It was soon found necessary to raise the top edge of the driver's windscreen to improve visibility on these and the subsequent D5s. Consequently the winding gear for the front destination display had to be moved to under the canopy. Previously the blinds could be changed from the cab, but now the conductor had to wind them from inside the upper saloon or externally. A footstep was therefore provided in the radiator grille.

With relatively heavy bodies and small engines, the AD2s were not over-endowed with power. Some of the Birmingham area garages did not retain their initial allocations for long, and the AD2s tended towards the flatter Leicester terrain, Stourbridge and the more rural areas. No 3101 loads at Banbury in the early 1950s, having received the windscreen modification and also vents in the front dome to improve airflow through the upper deck.

The relatively tranquil Banbury operations meant that the garage always fared well in the monthly accident statistics circulated throughout the territory, to the embarrassment of urban garages like Bearwood and Sutton Coldfield. Despite this, Mr Power was not keen on the rather detached Banbury operations and might well have approved of Stagecoach's transferring them to its Oxford subsidiary. The AD2s would have fitted in well with City of Oxford's largely AEC fleet and would have looked splendid in the latter's fine traditional livery. *The Transport Museum, Wythall*

the worse for slush. Beaming, she asked when we were to depart in a gushing received-pronunciation style. "As soon as possible," I replied. "Jolly good. I'll come with you to the Stag, then. I'm so pleased — I don't want to miss *Dick Barton.*"

Left: Brush-bodied BMMO D5 3551 in original condition with unmodified windscreen and front dome at Coleshill on route 168. It will return directly to Birmingham through Castle Bromwich while S8 3232, behind on the 165, will go via Marston Green and Sheldon. *R. T. Wilson / The Transport Museum, Wythall*

'About a third of the Dudley fleet were petrols with several "float" buses to ease the never-ending shortage of buses. The gear lever on nearly all the petrols moved in a gate, an aluminium mesh with a safety catch to prevent you from accidentally attempting to engage reverse at 30mph. This catch was a spring-loaded crank affair, with a knob about an inch in diameter for a handle. The objection to this arrangement was the difficulty of reaching down to floor level when seated. I found it awkward at 25 years of age, but greater minds had tackled the problem. Some genius of a driver had quite simply fastened a piece of string below the knob with the other end attached to the seat frame. By pulling the string, reverse could be easily engaged without the need for physical contortions.

'Enter the uninspiring shape of a Road Foreman. Road Foremen (officially known as Engineering Inspectors, but the old name stuck) were curious specimens of sub-humanity. They were hardly ever popular with bus crews, seeming to justify their existence by reporting absolutely everything mechanical that was in the slightest degree defective, especially if the driver could be blamed. This with a fleet still suffering from the ravages of wartime conditions.

'An elderly coachman told me about returning to his petrol bus and finding a Road Foreman peering inside. The vehicle had not been fitted officially with the offending string, so either it was removed or he would report the matter. All protests were in vain; out came the string.

'None of the petrol fleet (except a few coaches) was ever fitted with starters, and they weren't easy to coax into life at 5am on a dark frosty morning. At that time, the starting team would be preparing for action. There would be three standby drivers, with either the assistant foreman or a mechanic. Next, the rope is procured from the foreman's office, looking like the kind of thing used for mooring battle cruisers. Oh, and 20-size cigarette cartons.

'Now, with the mechanic adjusting the throttle and ignition as required with one hand, his other across the carburettor air intake, the engine is rotated a few times to suck in petrol. Then there is a mighty heave altogether on the rope, which might persuade the average engine to fire. No? Next time, and perhaps next again until suddenly away we go. His hand is replaced by the fag packet torn to size, a fast idle is set, and the next victim tackled. A temperamental beast would be left 'til last, extreme cases might need tow-starting. Finally the normal idling speed would be set and the cardboard choke removed. A driver should then find his bus started, warm and ready to drive.

'Among other foibles was a tendency for the petrols to overheat. One Bank Holiday Monday, I found myself on a Dudley to Kinver extra and had to take a pet hate of mine, petrol FEDD HA 9409. This detestable vehicle wasn't just a temperamental bus, and a pleasurable day's work became misery.

'We were in trouble even before reaching Brierley Hill. Ominous rumbling from the rad proclaimed that steam was well and truly up. I had been "advised" to watch the water level, and had borrowed a water can. An attempt at loosening the filler cap, with the aid of gloves, produced a great fountain of steam that enveloped the entire front of the vehicle. I then filled up, awaiting the next rumble. More time was lost in procuring further supplies of water. And that's how it was for the entire turn. You can imagine what the passengers thought of it; no doubt they were looking forward to the end of petrol rationing and to private transport.

'One day I tried to close the cab door of HA 9407. It was sagging on its hinges to such an extent that the catch was well out of line. So, as others before me had done, I gave it a hearty slam. Unfortunately this resulted in the driving mirror falling off. Time to go, so I did that trip with the mirror on my lap, occasionally poking it through the gap over the Klaxon horn to survey the road behind.

'The 140 to Birmingham was as hard to work as any on the Midland Red system, and too tightly timed for the distance. I had a petrol FEDD one day, and it was a good bus for pulling. We did better than expected for time until we stopped at the "Hall of Memory" in Birmingham. Car parking in Broad Street, even in those petrol-rationing days, did not allow me to pull in closely to the kerb and the bus was sufficiently far out to block following traffic. Then, to my shame, I stalled the engine. A lengthy queue was forming behind us and I had to suffer the indignity of jumping down from the cab and performing with the starting handle. In the opposite traffic stream came a Birmingham City Transport Daimler COG5. The young driver was quite obviously enjoying the spectacle to the full. As he came alongside he opened that unusual pivoted signalling window, and exhorted me to swing the handle. Considering that he had a bus with reliable Gardner engine, plus a self-starter, fluid transmission that wouldn't stall, servo brakes, enclosed cab and even trafficators, I felt that I was being taken advantage of.

'The entire oil-engined double-deck fleet at Dudley then consisted of members of the BHA 301-400 batch of FEDDs. Some lasted over 20 years, demonstrating the soundness of Metro-Cammell body construction. During wartime, the company had converted them to oil with SOS K or AEC engines (actually 7.58 litres, but AEC publicists liked 7.7). With nearly half a litre advantage, the SOS ones were better performers for acceleration and on hills, though the AECs were somewhat high-revving which, when on a level route like the 125/126, was worth having. Gearboxes and back axles had well and truly been mixed up with the desperate postwar maintenance situation. If you had a K-engined BHA still with rear axle intended for a petrol, you'd be short on speed but at least a gear better off for hill-climbing.

'I was aware that 1787 (BHA 385) was weak on the springs and had booked it off previously, but nothing had changed. I took it over at 6pm one Saturday evening on the 243, parked on the loading stand at Dudley, which was then on the railway bridge. In no time the bus was full and, as they occupied the top-deck seats, I saw with apprehension that the bus was leaning ever more to the nearside to such an extent as to contact the shelter. There was nothing else for it but to request those on top to get off and I then re-parked it. I booked the fault off in letters of fire.

'Back to the 140 and the road through Dixons Green and as far as Rowley Church was dreadful in the summer of 1947, following the ordeal of the worst winter of the century. So here we are with 1787, rapidly picking up at every stop. Most were going into Birmingham, and the upper deck filled quickly, of which I was soon made aware by the ominous swaying. The snaking motion on the bends was inducing slight nausea. We were halfway to Blackheath when, going round this left-hand bend, there was a sudden sharp crack like a rifle shot as the offside front main leaf snapped. We came to a stop within a few yards, with a smell of protesting rubber from the tyre as it was abraded by the wheel arch. By the mercy of providence, with that steep camber, it was the offside that had failed. I derived some indirect satisfaction from it all, as something now had to be done about the weak springs.

'A sinister ploy practised by the company was de-rating. A bus with the reputation of being a good performer would go for overhaul, yet on return be regularly booked off as pulling poor. It had of course been got at by Bearwood Fumblers, as one old Dudley driver called them, who had calibrated the pump to deliver a few percent less fuel, and were busy congratulating themselves upon the economy achieved. Before such treatment, a good bus with seated load might climb a hill in third gear. But after reduction it would only slog up in second at full revs with nothing

Below: D5 3491 will be off ahead of 3496 at the foot of Castle Hill, Dudley, *en route* to Stourbridge in 1960. *Patrick Kingston*

47

in hand. I always thought that more harm than good was ever done by this reprehensible practice.

'We had six 1934 BRR-class buses at Dudley, HA 9390-5. Usually they performed well, were good starters and their light weight allowed easy braking. But those cabs were too small — you did not so much get into them as put them on. Other sufferers were those with a portly waistline; you were subjected to unwelcome stomach massage from the steering wheel. You sat too high, of course, on top of that accursed petrol tank, and had to bend your neck forward to see below the upper edge of the windscreen. Everything was too close. Handbrake and gearlever were doomed to get in each other's way. There was so little room to reach down to the reverse catch that the piece of string was an absolute godsend.

'One of the regular homes of these BRRs was the D40 to Gornal Wood. This traversed a somewhat indirect route including an unmade-up bit of road known locally as "Cinder Bonk", which in fact was exactly what it was. As you drove along, a continuous cloud enveloped your vehicle. Advice was forthcoming from an old driver. It was straightforward going out, mostly downhill. Returning with an early morning load was not so simple. The bank was steeper than it looked, and those cinders had a dragging effect. Safest procedure, I was informed, was to stop at the bottom of the hill, engage second, and go up steadily without attempting gearchanges. I resigned myself that only Midland Red would dare to run services along such narrow lanes, back alleys and unmade roads.

'This Gornal service was included in what was known at Dudley as the "Owd Mon's List", a separate rota of single-deck turns worked by elderly or infirm conductors; men near retirement and not capable of working a double-deck.

'Among the float buses that I encountered occasionally were OLRs — prewar coaches demoted to stage service. With that narrow front entrance, they weren't really suitable for such duty, although the double-deck style low floor did offset this. Those new cabs were of course infinitely better than on, say, the BRRs, being roomy with good visibility; this was helped by absence of the fuel tank, which remained in its offside underfloor location. The original high gearing for coach work was unaltered so that acceleration from stops was somewhat leisurely. Whilst on loan to Dudley, they usually found a home on the 276 [Sedgley–James Bridge]. You could do a turn on one with a feeling of having enjoyed the day's work.

'In the summer of 1947 the company announced that a delivery of some new buses had taken place. Instead of allocating a new type entirely to one garage, there was to be a policy of fair shares for all. I entered the garage one day to find S6 3065 was the centre of attention, a shining harbinger of a rosy future, or so we innocently thought.

'I decided to reserve my opinion until I actually worked on it, and the opportunity came some weeks later when one Saturday I did a late relief turn on the 243 to Cradley

Heath. Having taken over, we reached Dudley Market Place to set down and pick up. It was gradually filtering through to me that they were taking an interminably long time to board and alight due to the high floor with three quite deep steps. There were good points. The bus was smooth and quiet, pulled well, and the servo-assisted brakes were more than adequate. At last we had the luxury of an adjustable seat, the fuel tank having been banished from the cab. The built-in heater and demister were further improvements. The lavish destination blinds were long overdue, after so many years of wretched stencils and boards.

'Then there was the serious menace of the anxious passenger invading the platform as a stop was approached, depriving you of nearside vision just when it was most needed. Cab visibility was inferior to anything previous. There was an additional artificial pillar too close to your nearside, caused by the saloon door always being hinged open, as there was not time to mess about opening and closing it — the folding power doors on later models would solve this. The offside door was a grave offender, hinged to a pillar set back from the windscreen pillar, with a tiny window between.

'Returning to double-deckers, though I still liked the old FEDD, it became clear to me that a rear entrance was notably quicker for loading and unloading, and all-important time was saved on short-distance runs. So let us turn to the AD2. In mid-1948 there descended upon Dudley garage three of these strikingly modern-looking AEC buses, 3113-5. Finding one on view, I sat in the cab and without hesitation condemned that high, wide bonnet for the poor nearside vision. The lower edge of the nearside valance was so low as to be almost level with the saloon window line, combining with the bonnet to give a tunnel-vision effect. Granted that they were under-engined, with only an old-fashioned 7.7-litre unit, and body weight increased by at least half a ton; yet I found them to be reasonable performers on level ground.

'A rumour arose among Dudley staff of yet more work-horses approaching, and they were to be Guys. It was all the more surprising when they appeared in the garage, well before the formal announcement in national transport publications. These were the latest Guy chassis with the biggest surprise — the 10.35-litre Meadows engine. With their Guy bodies several hundredweight lighter than the AD2s, the power-to-weight ratio, even when derated, was a driver's dream. They could climb almost anything, except trees and the sides of houses. Sadly, numerous problems were to arise until eventually all the Meadows were replaced by BMMO engines.

'I only knew them at their best; all those steep undulations were now ironed out. At first sight in the garage I knew from instinct that I would like them, and without doubt they were the best buses that I have ever driven. As you entered the cab, the striking impression was of truly excellent visibility. Mr Guy had copied the RT in lowering the rad by some 6in; after the porthole nearside vision of the AD2s, these Guys were a revelation.

'Digbeth, in the centre of Birmingham, had the biggest allocation of buses and coaches on the system. Transferring there, I met buses allocated during wartime, the 33 Daimler CWA6s with AEC 7.7-litre engines. Such refinements as flexible engine mountings were not to be found and at certain speeds vibration was painfully evident. I had of course met the AEC 7.7 in the BHA conversions, where they performed more successfully. The Daimlers had heavier bodies, and were less efficient with fluid transmission. One bus, 2511, was running with a Daimler engine. My outstanding memory was of the increased cab noise. Capacity was 8.6 litres, so 2511 could be a gear better than the others with a load but you needed earplugs.

'I also made the acquaintance of 1943 (CHA 2, or "Charlie Two"). Differences included fluid flywheel and pre-selective gearbox, similar to the CWA6s, which accounted for its presence with them at Digbeth. The quadrant mounted on the steering column took you by surprise. It was the usual Daimler product, yet fitted upside down on the left-hand side. Another idiosyncrasy concerned the turning circle. The steering had evidently not been set correctly to give the same lock on each side. I always booked the fault off, yet to my knowledge nothing was ever done.'

Above: Longer routes were the priority for the first double-deckers with platform doors, D5B class 3777-3876. Here 3801 loads in Station Street, Birmingham, before working the long 144 route to Malvern Wells. Fortunately the company had a fuel-filling point here, for the heavy D5Bs proved incapable of operating the 144 all day on a single tank of fuel. As soon as the lighter D7s came on the road, they were introduced to the 144, and the fuelling point was relinquished in December 1953. Satchwell's, behind the bus, had a large Midland Red clock on its wall for the benefit of staff and passengers. *R. T. Wilson / The Transport Museum, Wythall*

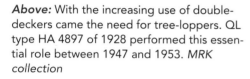

Above: With the increasing use of double-deckers came the need for tree-loppers. QL type HA 4897 of 1928 performed this essential role between 1947 and 1953. *MRK collection*

Below right: The bulk of the prewar buses were rebuilt by two firms, Aero & Engineering (Merseyside), of Hooton, and Nudd Bros & Lockyer, the latter handling most of the single-deckers included in the programme. The 1936 English Electric-bodied SONs had been unusual in having sliding doors, but, whilst the Nudd rebuilds retained these, the Hooton rebuilds received the typically BMMO porch-type entrances with folding doors. The sliding door on 1940 (CHA 564) therefore clearly identifies this as a Nudd rebuild. No 1940 was a long-term Worcester resident.

Most of Worcester's buses and coaches were kept at the familiar Padmore Street garage, but less well known was that 30 of the single-deckers were garaged overnight at premises in East Street, not mentioned in your trusty *Ian Allan ABC Midland Red.* East Street was also a body shop, capable of repairing up to three vehicles.

One Midland Red man told of the glee whenever a CHA-registered SON entered Carlyle's bodyshop for overhaul or repair. Apparently, on this batch only, money was apt to slip down between the sides and the floor. Each arriving CHA was therefore attacked profitably with a knife to winkle out the lost coins! *The Transport Museum, Wythall*

Above: The much more extensive body-renovation programme commenced in 1949, the vehicles involved retaining timber frames. These later rebuilt buses were obvious, sliding ventilators and rubber-mounted flush-glazed windows replacing the drop vents; the fancy mouldings below the windows also generally disappeared. Carlyle Works carried out the earliest rebuilds and set the pattern for the outside contractors to follow, though the style of sliding vent provided a recognition point. English Electric-bodied SON 1890 (CHA 514), rebuilt by Carlyle in April 1949, loads in Angel Place, Worcester. The company's enquiry office, with its handsome clock and discreet postwar fascia, is behind the shelter blessed with delicate wrought ironwork. *Michael H. C. Baker*

Back Numbers

Right: No 1631 (AHA 526) had its body rebuilt by Carlyle Works in November 1947, but its classic ON family lines remained largely as original, as seen in this view at Acocks Green, Birmingham, in the early postwar years. *G. H. Stone*

Below: CON 1505 (HA 9456), with Short body rebuilt by Carlyle Works in January 1949. *Alan D. Broughall*

Below: The CHA-registered SONs of 1936/7 had offside emergency doors allowing five seats across the rear, increasing seating capacity of the English Electric bodies to 39. Seen prior to rebuilding, 1926 (CHA 550) demonstrates the point at Pool Meadow, Coventry. *G. H. Stone*

Below: No 1916 (CHA 540) became the 38-seat exception after its original body was fire-damaged beyond repair in 1945. BMMO had an additional Short Bros body built in 1934, fitting it to MM class HA 5015 to form the solitary MON type. In 1937 the body was remounted on a Dennis Lancet II chassis (DHA 200) with Dennis four-cylinder diesel engine, no doubt purchased to satisfy the curiosity of the Experimental Department. The chassis was sold at the end of the year to South Wales Transport, the body being stored until reused on CHA 540. Seen at Hereford garage, it was rebuilt by Aero & Engineering (Merseyside), which firm's single-deck contracts came at the end of the refurbishment programme in 1951/2.
Michael H. C. Baker

Left: The first conversion of an ON-family vehicle to a service vehicle was 1934 prototype DON 1530 (HA 9481), seen on page 21, which became the tree-lopper based from 1951 at Leicester Southgate Street. For many years this veteran carried the only two-letter registration in the fleet, finally being scrapped in 1963. *R. F. Mack*

Right: Two SONs were rebuilt as full-front, dual-control training vehicles. Here a trainee gets to grips with Bearwood's CHA 551. *BMMO*

Below: The other dual-control SON trainer, DHA 696, was more camera-shy! *Alan D. Broughall*

Right: Routine rebuilds evidently went to Hooton, but this FEDD, 2341 (FHA 845), was far from straightforward and was rebuilt instead by Nudd in 1950. While, like most of its batch, working the 'Track' tramway-replacement service B87 from Oldbury garage it collided with a surviving tram standard and then demolished a shop front in Dudley Road, Tividale; two passengers were flung from the upper deck, which was torn open in the impact, and, tragically, one was killed. The rebuilt front end looked rather different, while the new sliding ventilators were of the style associated with Nudd rebuilds. This is the terminus at the Scott Arms, Great Barr, Birmingham. *MRK collection*

Left: An old chassis was kept at Carlyle Works to support any body temporarily separated from its own chassis. Here the Metro-Cammell body of 1755 (BHA 313) looks much too big for the slave chassis; the handbrake arrangement and the lack of tyre tread and inflation are interesting too! *G. H. Stone*

Above: Aero & Engineering (Merseyside), Hooton, initially handled double-deckers (sometimes the lower saloons only), rebuilding nearly all the Brush-bodied FEDDs, before moving on to single-decks. This January 1957 scene in Station Street, Birmingham, shows the very first Brush-bodied FEDD, 2119 (EHA 251) of 1938, on training duties after withdrawal the previous year, alongside 2255 (FHA 237) of 1939, obviously still very active on bus work, being ready to go all the way to Malvern Wells. Note that, over the years, the two buses have exchanged styles of radiator. *F. W. York / The Transport Museum, Wythall*

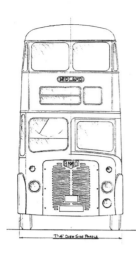
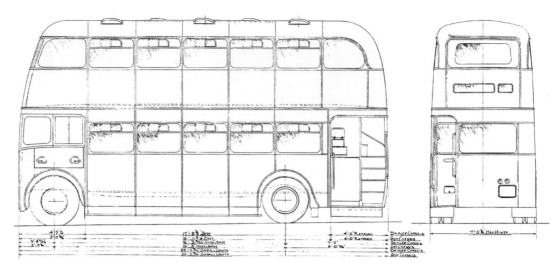

Above: This Metro-Cammell drawing is exceptionally interesting. The bus has most of the usual BMMO features, including the style of rear destination arrangements fitted to the earliest postwar buses, and complies with the 7ft 6in (rather than 8ft) width dimension. Note, however, that there are five bays rather than four, and that the forward facing windows are straight rather than arched. The plot thickens when you spot that the design was intended for Daimler and Guy chassis — clearly this drawing was intended for refurbishing the wartime buses. Straight lines meant simpler and cheaper components, which might have been a consideration for rebuilds. The five-bay construction is possibly explained by the fact the original body-bearers — and perhaps even the frames, with new window pans, fronts and rears effecting the transformation — were to have been retained; at the time it may not have been appreciated how much the wartime timber bodies had deteriorated. Metro-Cammell, specialising in metal bodies, would rapidly have lost interest had rectifications of the existing frames been mentioned. Simple modernisation, however, might have been acceptable; Met-Camm would later carry out similar work for Walsall Corporation.

Left: The rebuilding programme had to include the wartime bodies, those on Guy 2578 and Daimler 2546 being prototype rebuilds by Carlyle Works, completed in September 1949 and February 1950 respectively. The rebuilds of the wartime buses were considerable and indicate that they were expected to run for many more years. The exposed radiators were retained but given chrome-plated surrounds. New front wings, rubber-mounted windows, sliding ventilators and smooth, rounded rear roof domes all softened the austerity look. They also received postwar-style route and destination indicators, a modernisation not applied to the rebuilds of prewar buses.

In this view the prototype Carlyle-rebuilt Daimler, 2546, waits in the Bull Ring, Birmingham. This major terminus beneath St Martin's Church was blessed with a buffet for employees, erected during World War 2. The buffet was actually within the church-yard, thanks to the Church authorities, only 2ft from the nearest tombstone. *MRK collection*

Left: Following the example of the Carlyle prototype, Willowbrook rebuilt all the other Daimlers in 1950/1. The square-top side windows, with radiuses on the corners of the first and last windows only, were a distinctive Willowbrook feature of the time. *The Transport Museum, Wythall*

Right: Brush attended to the Guys with timber-framed Weymann and Park Royal bodies, in 1950/1, employing a quite different style of sliding vents. The Guy Arab II buses had their bonnets shortened to the Mk I position, and the cab fronts had a false panel added to make them flush with the radiator. This was 2564 in August 1950, its Weymann austerity features quite effectively disguised by the Brush rebuild. Rebuilding of the wartime bodies staved off the inevitable for only a short while; withdrawals began in earnest in 1954, and the wartime buses were all gone by 1957 — being outlived, for example, by most of the rebuilt FEDDs of 1938/9. Astonishingly, the Carlyle-rebuilt SOS DON alongside, 1703 (AHA 582), survives at Wythall. *R. Marshall*

Left: In 1951 the other wartime double-deckers were modernised, at Carlyle or Hooton, with built-up wings and postwar destination layout. Among the buses so treated were the six Duple-bodied Leyland TD7s of 1942; 2437 (GHA 791), here loading on the forecourt of Stourbridge Town railway station, was the only Duple rebuilt by Carlyle and retained the original thick pillar between the front upper-deck windows. In 1952/3 all nine TD7s were fitted with BMMO K-type diesel engines and BMMO gearboxes. *N. S. Stone, courtesy G. H. Stone*

8 | We don't carry passengers ...

Left: 'Aim at the tram!' SOS IM6 HA 6242 on driver-training duty passes BCT tram No 710 in Steelhouse Lane, central Birmingham. Built in 1931, though its Brush 34-seat body was a year older, it was one of the vehicles converted to run on producer-gas between 1942 and 1944 and would finally be withdrawn in 1952. The tram was also Brush-bodied. *The Transport Museum, Wythall*

The company removed its headquarters to Bearwood in 1914. The premises had begun transport life as horse bus stables but, as BMMO grew, more and more adjacent properties were acquired and added or redeveloped alongside the original land. Eventually Bearwood offices and garage were a fascinating architectural collection! It was at this extraordinary place that **R. J. (Dick) Nutt** began his Midland Red career. These are some of his memories.

Training

'The Midland Red was a thriving, progressive and prestigious organisation when I joined it as an engineering trainee on 30 August 1948 at a starting wage of £6 per week. I had already been through the intimidating business of an interview with God, ie Mr Donald M. Sinclair (DMS), the General Manager, which took place in what seemed to be the loft of the old Bearwood Road headquarters offices. Added to his severe manner was the off-putting fact that he had one glass eye. I found it impossible to figure which eye it was and which one to respond to while answering the questions he barked at me. It was all rather overpowering, and I was finally dismissed with the threat: "Please remember, we don't carry any passengers in this organisation." This was a management cliché of the time, and I wasn't sure he realised the pun; he didn't smile, and I didn't dare.

'On my first morning I reported to the Chief Engineer's Office for an induction talk. S. C. Vince was a very different character to Sinclair. He was a big, well-built man and always seemed to look at people through narrowed, half smiling eyes as though his thoughts were elsewhere, or perhaps it was to avoid the smoke from the pipe he often affected. My main memory of him was his high-speed, suicidal driving, which took no account of traffic lights at red: he simply drove straight through them, his theory being that if you went fast enough you'd beat the other chap across. My only memory of the interview with Vince was being told my training would include the Works Superintendent's Office under Mr George Plant, and that he was very much a rough diamond. That was rather intimidating, but George turned out to be a friendly, rather harassed old boy. He seemed to be always standing in the middle of his office beset with people wanting answers to impossible problems.

'Vince did not have Sinclair's forceful personality. Two powerful henchmen looked after the fleet operation side for him; one was the Assistant Chief Engineer, Mr Percy Geldard. His enthusiastic upholding of the previous Chief Engineer, Wyndham Shire, and his brutal regime was still well remembered.

'The man really in charge of running the fleet under Vince was the Rolling Stock Engineer, W. G. A. (Bill) Hall and he had a personality just as powerful as Sinclair. Well built with a military bearing he scared the living daylights out of his minions, the Garage Superintendents. The writer spent some time in the Rolling Stock office and this involved attending the regular Bearwood meetings of all garage supers, which Bill Hall presided over with an iron rod. These senior officers of the company, each a king in his own garage, sat around the long table smoking like chimneys, many trying to hide their shaking hands, awaiting the deliberately delayed entrance of the dominating Mr Hall. Those supers who had recently submitted a "B & D" form [*i.e.* a Breakdown & Delay report] were especially for the high-jump.

'Early on in my well-planned training programme it was made clear to me that the Traffic Department was out of bounds. Five years after Mr Sinclair had taken overall charge, the antagonism that existed between the founding fathers, Mr Wyndham Shire and Mr Power, the benevolent Traffic Manager, which had led to those in one half of the company being virtually forbidden to speak to the other half, was still making itself felt. True the barrier on the second floor dividing Traffic from Engineering had disappeared but the two departments still only really got together on the annual Sports Day.

'Shire's hard man philosophy was reflected in the vehicles he produced. Only when diesel engines were introduced were starter motors fitted. When I joined there were still many petrol-engined SOS vehicles in use. If I needed transport the Garage Foreman would deliberately allocate me an old QL type just for the pleasure of watching this wet-behind-the-ears laddie swing it to start. It didn't worry me, having been used to starting six-cylinder Bedford army trucks "on the handle" many times; it was just a matter of keeping one's thumb the right side of the handle ready for when she kicked-back. I could guess what this rugged old busman was thinking, watching this young Johnny-come-lately who was probably already on the same salary as himself.

'He might well be recalling the years taken to struggle from Fitter, at an unheated, poorly equipped outside garage, to Assistant Foreman, on almost permanent night-shift, responsible, on freezing winter nights, for a garage and forecourt full of buses, each one needing starting on the rope by himself and two mates every hour to stop them freezing up; anti-freeze was unheard of, Shire considering it much cheaper to have three men busting a gut. In between, the Assistant Foreman, with the help of a couple of fitters if he was lucky, would be expected to clear defects reported by drivers, throw in a brake shoe or piston change and have all vehicles allocated 'to turn' before first

Above: Prototype S13 3694 became known as S13 Mk 1, the remainder, 3877-3975, becoming S13 Mk 2. No 3877 was a 44-seat service bus, its Carlyle body assembled from parts supplied by Metal Sections Ltd — the first of many such kits to be purchased by BMMO for future production.
G. H. Stone

service around 5am. Tough as life had been for these loyal old company servants, they were never anything but helpful and supportive to me. Coming from the stuffy, insular Home Counties, it was a revelation and a great pleasure to find myself surrounded by warm-hearted Midlanders; everyone was friendly and good-natured, with lots of dignity and respect for others; this applied especially to the native "Brummies".

'My six-month training course started with spending time in all the administrative offices at Bearwood and then going through the extensive but ancient workshops. The very large internal bus parking space was surrounded on the south and east sides by a honeycomb of engineering offices and workshops, the latter having grown like Topsy since 1912 until the move to the splendid, newly built Central Works at Carlyle Road, Edgbaston, in 1953/4. It was hard to realize that this higgledy-piggledy collection of rooms and dark corners at Bearwood was the source of all Midland Red designs over some 40 years and two world wars. They certainly showed their age; wooden floors, benches and machines were old, black and oil-soaked, but everything was still serving its purpose well.

'However, present-day fire regulations would have closed the place down in minutes. The petrol and diesel re-fuelling pumps were a few yards in from the Rutland Road

Left: No 3879 was the first of the 40-seat dual-purpose S13s. Its body frame was assembled by Carlyle Works, almost entirely from Brush parts. All these early single-deckers with power doors had only a waist-high partition behind the driver, giving a very pleasant, airy *ambience*. *The Transport Museum, Wythall*

entrance and although the hoses were fitted with automatic cut-off nozzles, the floor was usually swimming in fuel oil, which nearly reached to the nearby entrance of the tinsmith's shop where blow torches and naked flame gas rings were being constantly used to repair radiators, fuel tanks etc. Next on the left was the dead-end passage to the engine test shop, with its copious petrol and diesel supplies, and immediately opposite was the blacksmith with his roaring forge with the uniform and clothing stores above. Moving on into the main garage, on the left were the stairs up to what had originally been the magneto overhaul shop, but the greater part of the work had become the servicing of diesel fuel pumps utilising two Hartridge re-calibration stands plentifully supplied with diesel and paraffin. Beyond was the cramped experimental workshop with no escape in case of fire, except through the fuel-laden magneto shop. Returning downstairs, the next along on the left was the large engine build and overhaul shop, and beyond that was a unique room where white metal was melted in a furnace and fed to a very clever centrifugal re-metalling machine designed in house to re-cast the bearing surfaces of petrol engine connecting rods. Above this was the works canteen. As if to complete this fire-fighter's nightmare, the garage would be jam-packed overnight with petrol and diesel buses, their fuel tanks full to the brim. The move of all the engineering departments to Carlyle Works, Edgbaston, was not before time.

'Until then, all mechanical engineering was concentrated at Bearwood. One of the latter's main functions had always been to assemble new, overhauled and experimental engines. The casting, machining and forging of most of the principal components was contracted out to Beans Industries, which became involved with manufacturing for Midland Red after the demise of the Bean motorcar in the 1920s.

'New engine components were lovingly assembled into either vertical or horizontal engines by half a dozen old-timers in a dedicated area of the engine shop. Older petrol and diesel engines of all types in the process of being over-hauled occupied the greater part of the engine shop. All the men, from Jack Blackham down worked together harmoniously — literally — as I found out returning from the canteen one afternoon. There was no piped "muzak" anywhere in Bearwood, so I could hardly believe my ears when the sound of a heavenly choir rose above the normal workshop din which I recognised as the cantata "Jesu, Joy of Man's Desiring" by Bach. On enquiring I was told the very pleasurable performance was thanks to those members of the engine shop who were part of the company choir rehearsing at their benches. They were all "good old boys", devoted to the company, who, when explaining a particular job to me, would start by saying, "Mr Sinclair will ask you all about this" or, "This is one of the things Mr Vince will expect you to know". In spite of the poor wages, minimal holidays and pension there was a powerful family feeling throughout the Midland Red then. There were no strikes and many men got to work very early, especially after the move to Carlyle Road, where a small club of early birds could always be found down in the rather nice new boiler room of a winter's morning, sometimes as early as 6.30am, eating their breakfast.

'All completed engines had to pass through Fred Haines' engine test shop. There were six engine test beds, carrying not only fairly modern power measuring Heenan & Froude DPX-4 dynamometers but also, perched on the end of each bench, an original electric drive motor removed from the last of the Tilling-Stevens petrol-electric buses of the 1912 era. These splendid old motors, which had probably covered hundreds of thousands of miles on the road, were indispensable as the means of motoring in petrol and diesel

Right: One S13 was very different from the comfortable dual-purpose vehicles that made up the majority of the type. Nudd-bodied 3919 had normal bus seats for just 32 passengers but had room for a further 28 standing — 20 more than usual. All the nearside seats were singles, while inward-facing seats were employed over the rear axle to give the necessary circulating space for the standees. Passengers entered at the front and left at the rear, both sets of doors being controlled by the driver. Having entered service in August 1952, 3919 was tested at various parts of the network, including a year at Leamington, but proved no more successful than other operators' contemporary attempts at a 'crush-load' single-decker. It settled at Shrewsbury, where it was to remain for the rest of its life, and in 1954 was rebuilt by Carlyle Works as a 44-seater. *The Transport Museum, Wythall*

engines (ie establishing oil pressure) and starting and acting as power absorbing generators for the reconditioned petrol engines that were still coming through. An end test bench carried a small DPX-3 dynamometer permanently coupled to a single cylinder diesel engine. This was the progenitor of one of the best ever diesel bus engines, the Midland Red's own 8-litre K type. After being used for one hundred and one experimental and development tests since the 1930s this little engine still carried the most recent experiment.

'This experimental work was the province of a curmudgeonly genius of a machinist, Arthur Parkes, who had his own very private workshop high up in the roof above the engine shop. After a first class apprenticeship at Belliss & Morcom, a leading marine engine maker, he joined the Midland Red in the 1920s specifically to manufacture and modify the various good, bad and indifferent prototype ideas generated by Wyndham Shire. The two worked closely together, and were in many ways similar, cantankerous characters. Arthur was probably one of the few people who talked without fear to Shire, partly brought about by Shire's enthusiasm for golf, which meant he was forever dreaming up new shapes of golf club heads. Working Saturday mornings, as we all did then, Arthur said he would just be finishing-up when Shire would appear at his elbow with yet another complex club head shape which he expected Arthur to produce ready for Sunday morning's game, and Arthur had little option but to put his cow-gown back on and work through the afternoon. Arthur didn't seem to resent this imposition.

'Arthur never sought to rise above the rank of foreman; he had his own shop, complete with lathes, milling and shaping machines and a skilled assistant, and was content with doing what he did so brilliantly. I got to know him quite well after joining the Experimental Department following my training course. Our mutual boss was Mr Jack Leslie Ransome BSc DCM MBE, another strong-minded character, but a splendid, understanding "gaffer" whom I developed a lifetime's affection for. He and Arthur got on in a guarded way. No-one gave Arthur orders, one asked for his help, which he then gave unstintingly, but always with a slightly supercilious air. Arthur considered no-one, but no-one, could do a job better than Arthur, and praise from him was praise indeed. He had no great opinion of the "high-ups", or anyone else for that matter. Sometimes Vince would bypass Mr Ransome, seemingly deliberately, since there was no love lost between them, and with great daring approach Arthur directly with some idea he had scribbled on a scrap of paper. Arthur only worked to professionally drawn engineering sketches at the very least, but he would listen silently while Vince explained his wants, leaving the offensive piece of paper with him. As Vince turned and walked out of the shop Arthur would pick up the paper and pretend to wipe his bottom on it.

'I knew only two other craftsmen like Arthur Parkes during my 46 years in engineering, and the quality and extreme precision of his handiwork outshone all. From its beginning in the 1930s he played a major part in making the Midland Red's K-type diesel engine one of the best of its kind. Arthur Parkes took the Design Office's drawings and, from the rough castings and forgings, proceeded to machine the crankshaft, camshaft, piston, cylinder and cylinder head, valves etc. He then assembled his handiwork into a running engine for test and development.

'Sounds easy but two items alone demonstrate his exceptional skill. The piston was not a straight lathe turning job. Its diameter had to vary elliptically, its length had to be barrel shaped and all external dimensions had to be within one ten-thousandth part of an inch. How Arthur machined out the deep, kidney-shaped chamber in the crown of the piston (from which the K engine took its name) he wouldn't say, but presumably he made up a form tool.

'Arthur could machine all 12 cams on a one-piece camshaft forging, which called for the developing of a master cam from the drawing, the making of a form-following attachment for his lathe and the precise setting of the angle of each cam using a dividing head.

'After six weeks at Bearwood, my training course took me to the Carlyle Road Workshops, situated on the west side of Edgbaston Reservoir, where new chassis and bus-body building and body overhaul had been established since the early 1920s. The premises consisted of two huge World War 1, Belfast-type hangars originally built to house the production of aircraft for the Royal Flying Corps, and in between were several ancient wooden sheds, one of which housed the body-drawing office. This was manned by Mr Lambert, body designer, who taught me to play chess in the lunch breaks, and his young assistant draughtsman, Ken Saunders; they were working on the design and construction of the next generation of all-metal bodies.

'My fortnight at Carlyle Road was mostly concerned with the body overhaul side which, in 1948, was just as much involved with wooden as metal-framed bodies. The Saw Mill still played an important role; it was surrounded by great piles of large, rough-sawn, carefully stacked planks: elm (for floors, mudguards and steps), ash (for pillars, waist and cant rails) and fir and parana pine (for internal mouldings), all undergoing long-term seasoning. In the workshops wooden bodies panelled in sheet steel and metal bodies panelled in sheet aluminium were being rebuilt and repaired side by side. Steel panels had to be laboriously attached to the wooden pillars by manually driving woodscrews with a pump-handled Archimedes screwdriver, and all slots in the screw heads had to be in line and aligned

with the nearest edge as a matter of pride. In contrast the new underfloor-engined vehicles had their aluminium panels pop-riveted to steel pillars using a powered riveting gun, and since pop-rivets have no slots there was nothing to align and the job was done in half the time.

'In the Panel Shop I was introduced to several skilled sheet metal workers, who could not only restore front or rear upper roof-end canopies after a driver had lost an argument with a low bridge, but also could produce prototype canopies with their double-contour corners and faired-in destination boxes. It was a real pleasure watching George Saint and his mate Johnny cut, shape and weld thin, 18-gauge aluminium sheets by hand so that the finished article looked as though it was a one-piece pressing. The biggest challenge, of course, was that this big, 8ft-wide work of art had to match up and fit exactly to its supporting frames and rails. Carlyle Works was in the throes of being rebuilt, and the splendid plan of raising double-deckers from below ground level for spray painting had yet to take shape. Buses were therefore still being hand-painted by a gang of men with paint brushes wobbling about on the top of huge, very high step ladders, having to do it all several times over applying primer, undercoat, finish coat and finally a coat of varnish.

'From Carlyle Road my training course took me to Digbeth, with its large allocation of buses and coaches of various makes on strength. Twelve days were spent in the "dock" and running pits, an unheated area at the far side of the huge space that was Digbeth garage. It was fairly rough and tough but the goodwill of the "Brummies", like Bert Daniels and Charlie Hawsford, made it worthwhile.

'After a week or so getting my hands dirty, I then went on to an extremely interesting series of night shifts spent in the Assistant Foreman's office at Digbeth helping to plan the next day's vehicle allocations and collating the previous

Left: A camera-shy vehicle was 3977, the LA (standing for Light Alloy), built entirely by BMMO and captured here at Carlyle Works. This combined all the evolutionary thinking then prevalent within Midland Red. The company's first chassisless vehicle since the solitary S5, it had independent-wishbone front suspension and the rubber rear suspension removed from trial vehicle 3405. Completed in 1951 to the new 30ft length, it was fitted with 44 seats and platform doors and featured an entirely new BMMO 10.5-litre engine, not surprisingly derated in this lightweight vehicle. Handed over for service in 1952, it was fitted with a 5.75-litre Leyland O.350 engine, which it retained until 1956, when it briefly reverted to a 10.5-litre unit before receiving a standard 8-litre BMMO. Delicensed at 10 years of age pending recertification, it was instead scrapped, but its many advanced features had paved the way for the S14 model. *G. H. Stone*

day's records of fuel and oil consumption, drivers' running reports, etc.

'The last four months of my training period were spent at Leicester, under the redoubtable Mr Raymond Tuft, in the offices and garage at Southgate Street and touring the area's garages, including Hinckley and Nuneaton. It was at Leicester that I learned about the battle for routes and passengers conducted by the Midland Red in the 1920s against other operators; it seems it was especially vicious in the East Midlands with Tuft playing a major part. One of the milder tricks was to run extra vehicles one in front and one behind a competitor to prevent any passengers being picked up. It was not unknown for one operator to "ditch" a rival's vehicle by forcing it off the road, punch-ups were common and it must have been a great relief when the 1930 Road Traffic Act put a stop to all that.

'The last weeks at Leicester were wholly spent being a trainee driver, which was a lot of fun. I was the only trainee at the time and Tom Grey, a very friendly type, was the only driving instructor. We both enjoyed getting out and about, covering many country miles around north and east Leicestershire, myself at the wheel while Tom occasionally roused himself to advise on the gear-changing techniques required with some of the older, petrol-engined buses the garage foreman had signed out to us. Getting it wrong at the very least produced blood-curdling, grating noises and at worst could snap off gear teeth that would then be carried round the other gears wrecking the gearbox, with the prospect, prewar, of instant dismissal on return to garage.

'Tom, to show his pleasure once we had got back to garage with a still functioning gearbox, would clown about. One of his music-hall tricks was rather unusual. He would be talking or listening in front of you and then suddenly disappear by instantly falling face down on the floor as though pole-axed from behind. Then, all in one movement, he would instantly spring upright again without any change of expression or break in the conversation. He had perfected the art of saving himself with his hands just before his nose hit the concrete and greatly enjoyed the consternation this caused.

Above: Vehicle testing was divided between public roads and the Motor Industry Research Association's proving-ground at Lindley, near Nuneaton. Midland Red made use of this facility soon after it opened; this particularly interesting view features the two prototype chassisless vehicles, S5 2579 (HHA 222) and LA 3977 (OHA 977), with construction of the banking for the high-speed track as a backdrop. There was also a half-mile stretch of Belgian pavé, along with a further concrete track with deep ridges at regular intervals. Among other tests, 3977 spent several days on these two tracks, making numerous trips. *Dick Nutt*

'After a couple of weeks with Tom, I was told to report to Bearwood for a pre-examination driving test under the eagle eye of Chief Driving Inspector Martin. The easy time at Leicester had not prepared me for the cut-and-thrust of Birmingham city centre traffic. Halfway down New Street I met my doom trying to squeeze past a lorry parked opposite a traffic island. A stentorian cry of "Stop, for C*****'s sake!" just saved me in time from collecting the lorry. That was the end of my test run; Mr Martin was not a happy man but showed some mercy. An intensive period of driving instruction around Birmingham city centre and the Black Country was prescribed.

'This really sharpened me up, not least having to face the oncoming trams that still ran the "wrong" way down Corporation Street. They reached quite a speed downhill and, as one drove uphill towards them, were mighty intimidating. Seeing my hesitation the instructor, Mr Hill, shouted: "Don't let them frighten you, aim to hit them with your offside front, go on, nearer, nearer!"

'It seemed like a recipe for disaster but he was right; I found that natural cowardice meant I missed the roaring, rattling monster at the last second, and it became quite fun scaring the tram drivers for a change. In the event I finally took my PSV test in Leicester; a doddle. I only drove a Midland Red bus in service with fare-paying passengers once, but having a licensed PSV badge was to prove essential. The company did not allow any vehicle to be taken onto the road without one, and the post I was about to be offered was going to involve much test-driving of buses over many miles.'

The Experimental Department

'In April 1949 on completion of what had become a seven-month training course, I accepted an offer of the post of Technical Assistant in the Experimental Department at the princely salary of £6 per week. My fellow trainees, Raymond Braithwaite and Peter Wood having been, respectively, a Major and a Lieutenant in the army, grumbled about the salary as we walked together to the bank to cash our weekly cheque, saying it was quite a drop from their army pay. I kept my own counsel; it was a very welcome increase from the £3 a week I'd left behind as a 23-year-old motor mechanic.

'In 1949 the Experimental Department occupied a large office divided into three on the ground floor front at Bearwood. Entry from the main garage gave onto a small laboratory, then a small office in which Jack Godfrey, Bob Moore and I had our desks with Mr Ransome's even smaller office, with its permanently open door, on the left. Jack Godfrey ran the office and was handling a trials programme of the then innovative low-viscosity, HD detergent engine oils which are now taken for granted. In 1949 the concept of seemingly dangerously thin oil that cleaned as well as lubricated an engine and reduced fuel consumption was a novel and very welcome idea. Various garages were running on the new oil, and a very close watch was kept on oil and fuel consumption, Jack and Bob collating the mountain of data produced. In addition Jack visited the garages involved to be sure oil leaks and faulty injection were not overlooked. When I joined, the trial was reaching its end, and I accompanied Jack to measure piston and bore wear and assess each engine's internal cleanliness.

The garage supers were not pleased with all the extra dismantling work this involved, but Mr R had made sure orders were issued by Bill Hall so there was no argument. The trial was a big success; low-viscosity, detergent oils were here to stay and Midland Red was a leader in their introduction. With the economics proved, our masters became drunk with success, went mad and ordered that low-viscosity oils be tried out in everything that moved. We were off again with wilder and wilder ideas, the ultimate being the filling of back-axle worm drives with engine oils having a viscosity as low as SAE5. This didn't last long, and the vehicles "enjoying" the treatment could be identified by the trail of leaking oil they left behind.'

Carlyle Works at last

'In 1950 the Engineering Department moved from Bearwood to the fine, brand-new, purpose-built building accessed via Carlyle Road. This huge, open-plan building, with various shops around its internal perimeter, was excellently planned and finished to a high standard and everything, big and small, was painted eau-de-nil, even down to hand tools. The move went very smoothly, and in the course of a few weeks everyone had been dragged out of the many dark corners that was Bearwood and found themselves working in spacious, well-lit surroundings, side-by-side under a single roof.

'From his upstairs office George Plant, Works Superintendent, his repertoire of choice Black Country technical sayings and similes still in full flow, was assisted by Peter Wood and newly joined Don Sheppard. Don was tall, dark and handsome, mighty cynical after the hardening experience of being called-up during the war to serve in the mines as a Bevin Boy (a hated form of National Service). Don later transferred to the Experimental Department, he and I sharing many adventures until Don returned to Central Workshops, finally taking on George Plant's mantle as Workshop Superintendent.

'First on the right as one entered the new building was the Experimental shop in which Arthur Parkes and his young assistant, Syd, were splendidly equipped with a lathe each, pillar drills, and a shaper, plus two engine test beds, one with a DPX4 dynamometer, the other with a DPX3. Ironically, there was no new Experimental office accommodation at Carlyle Road when Mr Ransome and I moved there on 2 October 1950. We were told to make ourselves at home in the ancient, original works canteen, a large wooden hut next to the reservoir. We took over the old kitchen, an area approximately 20ft-square, attached to which was the minute office previously used by the canteen manager. This became Mr Ransome's office to which he could happily retire and smoke his favourite Lambert & Butler's "rich, brown flakes" secure in the knowledge that the long trek to this remote corner of the Works would not appeal to certain of the 'high-ups'. This suited Mr R fine, he had a very low opinion of Vince and Geldard, having suffered under Percy's iron fist in his early years as driver and assistant foreman. Sadly, Mr Ransome's ire also extended to Mr Colley the Chief Designer, which resulted in almost no co-operation between Design and Experimental. Therefore, I had to tread carefully when visiting my friend Mr Jakeman and the other designer-draughtsmen, including "young" Stan Dews, who (to help his thought processes — he said) would now and again stand on his head between the drawing boards so that, amongst all the heads bowed over drawings, would suddenly appear a pair of legs.

'Mr Ransome was a character — pugnacious, tubby and somewhat vertically challenged, cast in the same mould as Winston Churchill, of variable temper but always highly supportive of those who worked for him. Known as Jack to past and close acquaintances and automatically addressed by us as "Sir" to his face and as Mr R. or "the gaffer" behind his back, Mr Ransome started with the Midland Red in the 1930s as a driver after years of being out of work following distinguished service in the 1914-18 war. He first of all joined the Royal Flying Corps and served with a squadron flying reconnaissance flights over the Western Front. After a period instructing and being injured in a flying training crash, Mr R. was transferred to an army unit on the Western Front and won the Distinguished Conduct Medal and the French Croix de Guerre, both for gallantry. I only found this out when Mr Vince mentioned the medals in his valedictory speech at Mr R.'s retirement party. Mr R., when pressed, said the awards were given for services rendered when he ordered his platoon to lie down in the mud so that the rest of the British army could keep their feet dry by marching over them. Visiting Mr R. some time after his retirement I was told in confidence that he got his medals for rescuing, under fire, a wounded man who was hung up on the wire in no-man's land.

'From just Mr R. and myself at Carlyle Road in 1950, our little band of technical assistants and staff had grown to seven by 1954, when, at last, we all moved from the old canteen into new quarters in the rebuilt central block. This also housed Albert Hobson and his noisy band of rivet-bashers, who were then beginning to turn out the chassis-less S14 incorporating coil spring independent front suspension, rubber rear suspension, disc brakes, etc. Over the intervening years our little group was renamed the Research and Development Department. Although called technical assistants, we actually functioned as project engineers. The Design office, under Mr Colley, designed the mechanicals, produced the drawings and had the proto-type made; we then took over the testing and development and, if everything proved satisfactory, the Design office released the production drawings for in-house assembly or for outside manufacture. Don Sheppard, Pat Patrick and I did most of the S14 prototype test and development work, liaising closely with outside suppliers like Metalastik, Girling, Rubery Owen, Lockheed, Hobbs Gearboxes and

Right: Having been damaged in a serious accident, the pioneer underfloor-engined bus, S1 1591 (BHA 1), proved irresistible to the boffins and in 1952 underwent further transformation, receiving a new front end. Brought right up to date, with power doors, it now lacked a conventional front grille, air being taken in through grilles below the windscreens. The new front was more cleanly styled than that of any postwar bus to date but did not sit comfortably with the prewar look of the rest of the vehicle. *Dick Nutt*

Right: No 3960 was at the cutting edge of brake technology in 1952, being fitted with discs on the front and rear wheels. Here it is undergoing the first brake-fade test, with Don Sheppard nearer the camera. Dick Nutt described Don as a good friend and a skilled driver but one who didn't know the meaning of fear, never slackening for blind bends or hidden hazards! Standing in front of 3960 is Bill Pollard, of Girling. *Dick Nutt*

many others. Each of us also had a motley collection of large and small projects, these covering the evaluation of products submitted by outside concerns or suggestions for improvements made by staff.

'Sometimes we were allocated a complete project to design, make and evaluate and one of mine started with my being given a compact radiator unit and instructions to fit it under BHA 1. This relic from the mid-1930s was in the process of being given a new front end following an accident, and I was told to come up with an effective heating system that would capture the hot air coming out of the radiator and duct it into the saloon in cold weather but divert it underneath the vehicle in summer temperatures. There was a pressing need for an efficient vehicle heating system by 1950. As in the car industry at that time the idea of using the waste heat from the cooling system to keep passengers warm was only just beginning to be taken seriously. The advent of powered, platform doors increased the interest in providing heating for passengers.

'Midland Red had engaged Clayton Dewandre to devise a heating system for single-deckers and coaches. One design was their large, single L-type heater unit which was fitted underfloor. Its blower drew outside air through a small grille situated at waist level halfway down the side of the vehicle, unfortunately an area of low pressure. The air then passed through coils heated by the engine's cooling water and into a duct running the length of the saloon. The ducting losses meant that warm airflow, especially at the back, was practically non-existent. Clayton Dewandre appointed Mr Scott, one of its heating engineers, to work with us.

'The first move was to see how bad the situation was, and he and I were detailed to catch C1 coach 3339, fitted with an L-type heater, which was rostered for London Victoria and return, departing Digbeth at 8am on Wednesday 13 February 1952. The winter of 1951/2 had been bitterly cold, and the 13th was no exception. We started in snow and it just got colder and colder. At Aylesbury the outside air temperature was six degrees below freezing. No M1 motorway then, just a long drag, with both of us unobtrusively taking interior saloon temperatures until it became clear we were wasting our time. So we sat and suffered along with the other passengers until we reached Victoria. Even though I'd worn fleece-lined boots my feet felt like blocks of ice. As we disembarked on returning back to Digbeth, I showed the driver my letter of authority to take over and drive the coach back to Carlyle Road. He said: "If I'd known earlier I would have handed over the driving to you and taken it easy."

'This experience made me keen to make a success of the BHA 1 underfloor heat-exchanger scheme and by adopting a plain front, with air inlets positioned at a point of high pressure just below the windscreens and with an engine-driven fan in the ducting behind the underfloor radiator, a good airflow and a respectable saloon temperature were achieved. A simple shutter positioned in the ducting and controlled by a lever alongside the driver allowed an infinitely variable setting for hot air to flow into the saloon or under the vehicle and could have lent itself to automatic temperature control in the future.

'Hindsight shows that we were never going to get enough heat out of the engine's cooling water, especially in winter, without fitting a high-temperature thermostat into a system that bypassed the radiator, plus pressurising the system. Such a major modification, at the time, would have been an expense too far. If only one of us had stopped panicking, sat down and done some quiet thinking, it would also have become obvious that the whole diesel-engined fleet was operating overcooled to the detriment of fuel economy and, probably, engine life and lubricating oil consumption. Just one more mile per gallon would have been worth the expenditure.

'Thanks to the big cast radiator, even on hot summer days, no matter how many times we climbed Hopton and Angel Bank — first-gear grinds to the top of Clee Hill — there were never any overheating problems. So long as coach drivers didn't come back from Scottish or Welsh tours with reports of radiators boiling over, no one gave the subject much thought.

'Not that we had the test equipment to properly assess cooling performance. I don't think Mr Ransome ever had an equipment budget; nothing new was ever added to our pathetic little collection of antiques. We could rustle up one stopwatch, one thermocouple unit, 12 glass thermometers, a hand-held anemometer which measured air flow, a row of thermal paints (which changed colour at specific temperatures when painted for example on a brake drum), a linen, 100ft tape measure, one Tapley Brake Meter and a marvellously Heath Robinson means of measuring brake stopping distance made by Arthur Parkes in the distant past; anything else you wanted you made yourself.

'In 1952 disc-brake development began with Girling's designers and testing engineers using S13 3960. Although it was not my project I acted as accompanying driver and stand-in if Don was absent. The first Girling all-round disc brake system was a revelation after living with drum brakes.

'However, a trip out to Clee Hill on 22 December 1952, and several descents of Angel Bank revealed a major problem. The brakes disappeared completely! This wasn't caused by any mechanical shortcoming or deterioration of the friction material, but was due to the brake fluid boiling and turning from a liquid into a gas, resulting in the brake pedal going right to the floor. Fortunately the independent handbrake system proved very effective. Morale was severely dented, but the Girling engineers were not all that surprised, having been involved with the new Grand Prix racing disc-brake system fitted to Britain's then great white hope, the BRM racing car pioneered by Raymond Mays. It also was suffering brake loss problems, but none of the various palliatives seemed like a proper solution.

'A return to the drawing board and a review of the design ensued. The callipers were not fitted with a single pad as in today's design: each calliper carried six, 1¼in-thick circular pads, fronts being 2¼in in diameter, rears 2in. Aluminium pistons of the same diameter acted over the whole of the area of the back of each pad, and such close surface contact unfortunately provided an excellent conduction path for heat to pass directly into the operating fluid. The solution was simple and wholly effective: the contact area between piston and pad was greatly reduced, so reducing the heat conduction path and introducing a thin, but very important layer of still air between piston and pad.

'This modification took time to produce and meanwhile Don, myself and the Girling installation engineer Bill Pollard enjoyed the summer of 1953 trying out the palliatives and searching for a fade testing venue to use for the final proving tests, compliance with which would enable disc brakes to be signed-off as safe for use anywhere in Great Britain. This involved finding the steepest and longest gradients likely to be encountered by coaches on tour, and the approach from the north on the A470 to the village of Dinas Mawddwy in North Wales fitted the bill very well.'

Above: The long journey to an advanced lightweight chassis-less bus finally ended in 1953 with S14 prototype 4178. This photograph was taken in North Wales, during a final brake-fade proving trip to Dinas Mawddwy in July 1953, following which the Girling disc-brake system was accepted as fit for purpose. From left to right are Girling engineers George Wood and Bill Pollard, BMMO Experimental Engineer Jack Ransome and two of his recent arrivals in the Experimental Department, Jim Pearson and Ken Worrall. Principally involved in the problem-solving were Dick Nutt (behind the camera) and Bill Pollard, along with Don Sheppard, who had recently moved over to the Workshop Superintendent's office.

No 4178, seen here with a rather crude grille, weighed just over 5 tons — a saving of 2 tons over the preceding S13. The S14 featured disc brakes on all wheels — the first production PSV in the UK so equipped — and a steel body structure with the outer panelling in light alloy and glass fibre. Single rear wheels were deemed sufficient, contributing to the weight saving.

Midland Red was a pioneer in employing light fibreglass in the construction of its buses. When showing important visitors around the Works Mr Vince would ensure that a fibreglass corner panel was handy and give it a mighty bash with a large balk of timber. This was very impressive at the time, the panel surviving with barely a scratch in a situation where an aluminium panel would have crumpled. BMMO's continuing development work increased the proportion of this material in later buses, eventually extending to one-piece moulded roofs. *Dick Nutt*

9 | Property matters

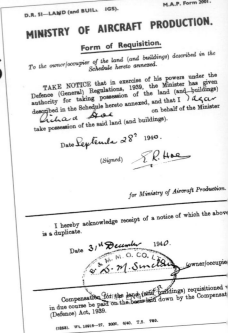

These developments were the zenith of the company's many property activities. Ensuring that the operating fleet was properly maintained in suitable premises had long been a priority, and Midland Red must have been very proud of its building stock, housing nearly 1,500 vehicles by the outbreak of World War 2 in 1939.

After the fall of France in 1940, the Ministry of Aircraft Production urgently requisitioned portions of several garages for the manufacture of components or sub-assemblies. Mr Sinclair, the new Chief Engineer, had queried with Austin Aero why it needed to take accommodation required to run works' bus services, essential to the war effort. He was invited to the factory and shown the new Stirling bomber plane. Austin pointed out that few companies owned buildings with the necessary headroom to enable certain parts to be assembled. Fewer still had doorways or accesses that enabled the structures to be extracted after assembly. At Bromsgrove spare space was available, and the company was happy to help, receiving in the process a good rental. Elsewhere there was some consternation.

One morning in November 1940, Mr Power arrived at work to find Mr Carleton Dyer of the Ministry of Aircraft Production waiting for him, to discuss Hinckley and Coalville garages. Things plainly did not go well as these extracts of Mr Power's letter to the Regional Traffic Commissioner show:

'To cut a long story short, he told me after an hour's argument, that Lord Beaverbrook was going to have the garages at once …

'Lord Beaverbrook says that the forces run aeroplanes and army lorries from fields, roads and waste ground and we must run buses in the same way.

'It is useless arguing any further with people like that and the only thing to do is refuse to hand over the premises and

Above: Bromsgrove enquiry office in the O. C. Power era.
The Transport Museum, Wythall

In 1953 a former private hospital in Vernon Road, Edgbaston, Birmingham, became the registered offices, although the Traffic and Staff Departments were to remain at Bearwood for nearly 20 years longer. Appropriately renamed Midland House, it conveniently adjoined the Carlyle Road central workshops.

The big Golden Jubilee event in 1954 marked the reopening, on 25 November, of Carlyle Works, steadily extensively reconstructed since the war. Its renaming as Central Works was not entirely convincing, as the old name continued in common use. BMMO was particularly proud of the Paint Spraying Booth in which a double-decker would be lowered 11ft below floor level and gradually raised as it was spray-painted — a revolutionary process at the time.

see what they will do. I understand from you that you will send us letters telling us not to hand over the garages to anyone, which we can give to the officials in charge at Hinckley and Coalville.'

Mr Carleton Dyer got his bus garages, including the whole of the Hinckley premises. Notification to part-occupy Coalville garage for a second time arrived in March 1943. Mr Sinclair's letter of protest included reference to the company requiring the space for the operation of producer-gas vehicles. The inability to house the producer-gas units and their servicing plant meant it would be unable to carry out the conversion being urged in the national interest by the Ministry of War Transport. A good excuse! Protests could work, however. The Air Ministry agreed in April 1941 to release Hereford from requisition.

Shrewsbury garage was also largely given over to aircraft production. The company stressed the need for replacement premises and eventually obtained, from 25 November 1940, the use of a timber shed for 15 buses, owned by Salop Timber near Abbey Foregate at Old Coleham, which remained in use until 28 February 1946. This was clearly inferior to the company garage in Ditherington. A departmental letter dated 12 February 1941 began: 'I endeavoured to visit the Old Coleham Garage, but at the moment access can only be gained by boat ...'

Going through the records for each garage, one generally finds a reference around 1943 to the construction of a lavatory for conductresses — female staff being almost unknown outside of the big offices until then.

The immense passenger growth following the end of the War in 1945 brought considerable pressure on garage space. Where possible, double-deck vehicles were introduced, and a major programme of building and extending garages was undertaken. These bore no resemblance to their prewar counterparts but, again, a clear house-style linked most of them.

Some properties took a long time to achieve. The land for the new garage in Myton Road, Leamington, was acquired in 1936. With nothing on the ground by the outbreak of World War 2, staff were permitted to plant allotments. Most gradually fell out of use by 1955, when those remaining were given notice to quit. Postwar building restrictions and more pressing requirements elsewhere had delayed matters, but the new garage was at last opened on 1 September 1957.

Mr Sinclair's determination that Midland Red should maintain the highest standards extended to other properties. For example, Traffic Manager Richard Brandon was on the receiving end of this departmental letter from Mr Sinclair, who evidently did not like the showmanship surviving from Mr Power's era:

'Passing through Bromsgrove today, I could not but be struck by the rather cheap look of our Enquiry Office in Bromsgrove. It looks more like someone's ice-cream parlour than a passenger enquiry office, and I think that something

Above: Stourbridge enquiry office and travel bureau c1959, after reconstruction of the garage frontage. *BMMO*

ought to be done to clean up the exterior and give it a more dignified appearance.

'I suggest that the existing enamel plates should be scrapped, and the whole frontage re-arranged.'

A new Bromsgrove booking and enquiry office opened in June 1951.

Private houses also formed part of the property portfolio. A house in Carlyle Road, Birmingham, was purchased, amongst other things, to save the cost of a night watchman. A house was built in 1923 in Washington Street, Worcester, almost adjoining East Street garage. Mr Shire wrote: 'From the Company's point of view it will be very advantageous for us to have our Foreman on the spot at our beck and call, any time, day or night.'

Other properties included several staff hostels introduced after World War 2. It had already become necessary, in some areas, to recruit staff from outside the Midlands, but the severe shortage of living accommodation was a problem. Around 30 single men were accommodated in each hostel, which had lounges and 'a resident warden and his wife' whose duties included preparing meals.

Birmingham's centrally located Digbeth garage had opened in 1929, part being used as a coach station. The postwar growth caused particular pressure and large numbers of buses had to be open-parked. Around two acres of land in Marshall Lake Road, Shirley were acquired in 1947 on a 99-year lease for a new garage, and there was a costly option of converting Digbeth to a two-level garage when it was reconstructed. The Shirley idea did not proceed, as it was feared that platform staff recruitment would be a problem, already revealing itself elsewhere. The takeover of part of the Walsall Road group of services by Birmingham City Transport took most of the steam out of the problem, although Digbeth continued to have an overflow yard; an ever-changing location as the inner areas of Birmingham were redeveloped. The garage itself was rebuilt in 1958 as an orthodox one-level structure, with coach passenger facilities within a new multi-storey office block on the Digbeth frontage.

IF YOU WISH TO TRAVEL BY ROAD
CONSULT—
MIDLAND RED
THE FRIENDLY "MIDLAND RED"

Above: Did the decision to buy Leylands for Stratford Blue eventually influence BMMO in choosing Leyland as its secondary supplier from 1952? With big engines and synchromesh gearboxes but few grabrails inside, the all-Leyland PD2s forming the LD8 class were loved by drivers and loathed by conductors. They made great open-road buses and were well suited to garages like Digbeth, Kidderminster, Leamington and Ludlow. At one time Digbeth operated no fewer than 35, and a cluster of them was a familiar sight in the Bull Ring beneath St Martin's Church, where 4040 and 4020 are seen loading when new. *Alan B. Cross*

Following the LA prototype single-decker, Midland Red enthusiastically developed lightweight vehicles. The last true 'heavyweights' were 100 double-deckers built completely by Leyland, classified LD8 and delivered in 1952/3 to meet urgent fleet renewal, and 75 BMMO coaches built in 1953/4.

Carlyle Works produced its first fibreglass panel in July 1953. From then on, the Plastic Department would produce more and more parts in this light, tough material. This was important because BMMO was about to enter quantity production of its own bus bodies.

Adding to the Golden Jubilee in 1954, Mr Sinclair revealed the new S14 prototype, 4178. This was the culmination of development with the S5 and LA chassisless experimental vehicles. No 4178 included chassisless

Below: The 75 coaches built in 1953/4 comprised 63 37-seat C3 long-distance service coaches and 12 32-seat C4 tour vehicles, all built to the 30x8ft dimensions. First to be bodied was a C4, by Carlyle Works. The C3s were bodied by Willowbrook, and the remaining C4s by Alexander; they all looked remarkably alike, save that the C4s had glazed panels in the roofs to aid sightseeing. Entrance doors remained in the centre, so the coveted front nearside seats remained. In this view low sunshine highlights the upholstery of C3 4185. *G. H. Stone*

Above: D7 chassis under construction in the Chassis Production Shop at Carlyle Works. *BMMO*

Right: A new D7 chassis undergoes road-testing in February 1958. *G. H. Stone*

construction, independent front suspension and toggle-link rear suspension (both making extensive use of rubber), disc brakes on all wheels and a disc-transmission handbrake. The BMMO 8-litre engine had evolved into the KL type, of which a horizontal version was fitted to the S14. Fully automatic transmission was a major innovation.

Mr Sinclair declared: *'With this design we believe we have taken a big step near the ideal bus at which we are constantly aiming. We have combined strength with lightness of weight to make for fuel economy, lower maintenance costs and greater passenger comfort.'*

The S14 was so light that single rear wheels were sufficient, but it rode like a truck. The S14s were designed to seat 44, while a slightly heavier variant, the S15, had 40 seats to dual-purpose standard and reverted to twin rear

wheels. Only a few S14s were built with automatic transmission, being replaced by traditional constant-mesh gearboxes, fitted from new to the remainder. S15s were loaned in 1957/8 to fellow BET operators South Wales, Northern General, Maidstone & District and Potteries to compare with their usual purchases. If only they had become customers, the subsequent history of British bus production may have been quite different!

Alongside the S14s and S15s, the Works manufactured 350 BMMO D7 double-deck chassis with KL engines and constant-mesh gearboxes, on which Metro-Cammell built lightweight bodies. The staff magazine reported in 1958 that 1,400 buses carried one or more experimental items, ranging from air-cooled engines to brake parts — in a fleet of just under 1,900 vehicles.

Left: Turning the scales at just over 7 tons, Midland Red's D7 double-decker was a ton lighter than its D5B predecessor, despite being a foot longer to take advantage of relaxed length restrictions. No 4750, new in 1957, was one of just two D7s allocated new to Hereford and was still working there on Saturday 13 June 1970 when seen outside St Peter's Church. *Malcolm Keeley*

Below: S14 4556 at Bearwood bus station displays the brown paint familiar throughout the interiors of BMMO service buses before the D9 generation. *The Transport Museum, Wythall*

Right: Midland Red buses bristled with test features. Instead of the usual sliders S14 4326 has hopper ventilators, as chosen later for the S15 vehicles, but with a push-out extractor vent in the rearmost bay. *G. H. Stone*

Left: No, not an Evesham local. S15 4646, in black-roof dual-purpose livery, demonstrates BMMO ideas to Maidstone & District, then standardising on AEC Reliances. *B. W. Ware*

Right: The early-postwar underfloor-engined single-deckers were well ahead of their time but nevertheless began to look old-fashioned alongside later buses. In 1957/8 three S8s received S15 front ends with power doors and cab access via the saloon. No 3237 was rebuilt by Carlyle Works, and 3217/41 by Willowbrook, the trio being redesignated S8 Mk1. At the same time they were re-trimmed in red moquette and leathercloth, which replaced the earlier brown-based scheme, and some other S8s were similarly treated. Here 3217 and its crew prepare to leave Rugby garage in March 1959. *Patrick Kingston*

11 | Twenty-five years with Midland Red

Stan Letts' long career with Midland Red was primarily office-based, but the shortage of platform staff gave him a great opportunity to know his industry in much greater depth.

On being a Midland Red trainee

'Way back in 1948, fresh from school, I joined the Midland Red, and on account of a good grade in the then School Certificate, I was taken on as a Company Trainee. This was a scheme practised by BET Federation companies where potential management personnel were put on a three-year course, going through every aspect of a bus company's work, with a view to eventual management-level appointments. This was usually offered to university graduates and

Above: Three amigos. Messrs T. Hawtin, N. Andrews and W. S. Webb, drivers at Banbury with a century of Midland Red service between them, photographed for the *Staff Bulletin* in 1953. We encountered Mr Webb 30 years earlier, on page 7. *BMMO*

former officers of the Armed Services. However, a similar course was offered purely at local company level for "bright" youngsters, of which the Midland Red management must have thought I was one.

'Halfway through the three-year course I had to do my statutory stint of National Service in the Royal Air Force. After my demob leave I reported back to the Bearwood offices of Midland Red to complete my training schedule. My time as a Clerical Trainee included the Staff Department, seeing how staff records were kept; the Engineering Department learning how Stores Control was exercised; the Accounts Department watching how the wages were made up. In the last case I marvelled at how the staff stayed sane with the same rigid routine week in, week out but most of the training only induced yawns.

'What really took the biscuit, however, was the Parcels Department. Its business was conducted from Dudley Street, Birmingham, in offices that had been by-passed by time. Antique furniture was littered with dusty ledgers. In this time warp I was given the monumentally boring task of checking stocks of the various values of parcel tickets.

'It was small wonder that following this week of galloping tedium I was summoned to a grim-faced Staff Manager, who was in charge of trainees and their courses. I received a sound ticking-off for not displaying any interest in the workings of the Parcels Department, and that if I didn't mend my ways, I would be taken off the course. I didn't have to mend my ways, because by then I was learning about the Timetables Office, to which it was my ambition to belong, and to which I could give every ounce of enthusiasm.'

Out into the sticks

'The final part of the training course consisted of the trainee being sent out for a six-month spell with a Divisional Superintendent. This was the bit I dreaded, because no way did I relish the thought of having to find digs in Leicester or Hereford or Shrewsbury. Not that I have anything against those fine towns — there were just too many miles between them and Mum's home cooking.

'However, much to my relief I learnt that I was to spend this part of my course among Black Country folk. The Divisional Superintendent was not enamoured with having a trainee under his feet and disturbing the even tenor of his

Right: Warwick Market Place in 1955, with, from left to right, Driver Jim Wimbush, Conductor George Inglis, Driver Ron Cotton and Conductor Dennis Burke. Alongside CON 1632 (AHA 527) — shortly to become the company's publicity vehicle — is SON 2429 (GHA 348). *Patrick Kingston*

own little fiefdom. So, a quarter of an hour after I had reported to his Dudley office, I was on my way to spend my allotted time at Cradley Heath garage. Here I really learnt about running a bus company from the "sharp end". It taught me that operating garages are the backbone of any bus company, while those luxuriating in their cosy head offices are only (often quite dispensable) support staff. With that lesson in mind I never, throughout my career, seriously pulled "Head Office" rank over local people (although on an odd occasion I did so for a little bit of innocent fun). What a happy time that was. Everyone — inspectors, office staff, schedules inspectors, drivers, conductors — all were so friendly towards me. And I could get home for tea!'

The Knowledge

'Having completed the Midland Red training scheme, I was asked which department took my fancy, and of course I opted for the Timetables Department. However, the Midland Red was still, in those days, run on somewhat military lines. Thus instead I found myself behind the counter of the company's main Worcester Street booking office in Birmingham city centre.

'Depending upon the season, this could be extremely hectic or incredibly tedious. At busy times, when bookings opened for the summer express services, we could have queues stretching out into the street. We booked for places all over the country. A regular passenger was a forthright elderly lady, a frequent traveller on the Yorkshire Traction service to Barnsley, who would demand of the booking clerk: "Ah want ticket on t' Yorkshire *Tractor*."

'A seaside destination often requested was Swanage, which wasn't served by any express service. Never fazed, we clerks would issue them with tickets on the direct Bournemouth service. They seemed quite impressed when we told them to change onto Hants & Dorset service 6, every half-hour from Bournemouth. Behind the counter we

had an up-to-date timetable book of every major operator in the country. No matter what the destination, we could get the passenger there — we had acquired our own brand of "the knowledge".

'A year there had proved very interesting but I became aware that the next year was just going to be a re-run of what I had been through, and the prospects were those of a dead-end job. It was surely not for someone who had been through such a comprehensive training scheme. So I submitted a request to the Traffic Manager, repeating my preference for a full-time job in the Timetables Office.

'I heard nothing for some weeks. Then, at opening time one Monday morning, before the general public started to come through the doors, a young man walked in asking for the head man, saying that he had "come to replace a Mr Letts, who was to report to the Timetables Office at Bearwood". That's exactly how I got to know of my move! Just like the military, the chap concerned was the last to know.

'During my short stay in the Timetables Office in my time on the Training Scheme, I had entertained hopes that not only would I eventually be given a job in that department but would be allocated to a "nice" area of the company's operations. I had always been rather fond of Herefordshire, and to have Hereford garage within my "parish" would, I thought, have been quite delightful. Worcester or Evesham also had pleasantly bucolic associations in my mind. At the other end of the scale the Black Country was a bit on the rough-and-ready side (a heavy industrial conurbation with lots of works buses and all that), while the really local stuff at Bearwood garage and (even worse) Oldbury garage held no attraction at all. Who would wish to take responsibility for all those grotty Smethwick works buses?

'Yes, you've guessed — the military mentality struck again. I was welcomed into the Timetables Office by the Timetables Superintendent, who informed me that I would be assisting on the Black Country section, and to get me eased in gently, my "own" garages would be Bearwood and Oldbury! The irony is that it proved to be one of the best things that happened to me. It became a source of pride that I became one of the very few who really knew where all those complicated Smethwick area works buses ran. I was the only one in the office who could compile a timetable and the attendant bus-working timetables, and afterwards look out of the office window onto the Bearwood Road and see my work actually happening! The Black Country became, as it were, my spiritual home and I was very contented to be associated with it.

On goes the cashbag

'The company was experiencing a grave shortage of plat-form staff and, by the 1950s, office staff were actually undertaking evening and weekend conducting duties. Often mornings would see men holding "post-mortems" on their previous evenings' duties. These conversations fascinated me, and I resolved to get involved myself, so I saw the man in charge; I was allowed to become the first part-timer at Bearwood garage. Due to the fact that I had been through the Conducting School as a Company Trainee, I skipped that stage, and went straight onto dealing with the public, but under the care of long-service experienced conductors. I think it was after about half-a-dozen evening stints, and one full Saturday stint as a trainee that I was deemed competent to go out on my own.

'The day arrived for my first "real" shift. It was a middle duty on a Saturday, out of garage at mid-day for eight hours on the 119 Walsall Road service between Birmingham and Scott Arms — a Birmingham Corporation route worked by Midland Red since the year dot. But a brick had been dropped, and I had been paired with a driver whose own first day on the road it was.

'In our FHA-series FEDD we were innocents in the rat race, and whilst the old hands got up to all kinds of trickery, we only knew how to work strictly to the running card. I spent quite some time on the platform observing all the other buses running with full standing loads — and I didn't have a standing passenger all day. This was a lesson that was thereafter to stand me in unfailingly good stead. The easy way to do the job is to do it properly. I never deviated from that principle thereafter.'

The dreaded Verometer

'Bearwood in winter, without all its summer coach work, offered only sparse pickings for part-timers. I was soon snapped up by Cradley Heath for regular Saturday conducting duties. I had been spoilt by the nice easy Setright ticket machines at Bearwood, and now I was faced with the formidable lump of machinery that was the Clayton-Harris Verometer. It was clumsy. You could always tell a Midland Red conductor based at a garage equipped with Verometers — his knuckles were raw from constant grazes.

Above: Stan's early conducting days included spells on FEDDs on the 243/4, although this is not him! Final-series FEDD 2358 was allocated to Cradley Heath from 1956 to 1960. *Patrick Kingston*

'I well remember my first Saturday shift. It was snowing hard, and I was on the busy 243 between Cradley Heath and Dudley (on a Saturday, combined with the through 244 workings to Wednesbury, the frequency was every four minutes). There was no heating on the old BHA-series FEDDs, which were the mainstay of that route, but one was far too busy to notice the cold.

'On the following Monday I was in the Waybill Office, and Gladys, the matriarch in charge, said to me something like: "Yo was on'y on 243s — that am easy. Yo wairt till yo'm on the tew fower fower to Wensbry. Yo'll soon find art wot waerk really am on that un — it's bin knowd fer strong men ter weep!"

'And so the time eventually came. The shift, again on an old BHA, started with a round-trip on the "easy" 243 to Dudley. In view of a potentially busy 244 trip in front of me I loaded my Verometer with a new ticket roll. Off we set from Cradley Heath High Street. It was at Great Bridge that my ticket roll gave notice that it was getting to the end, 400 tickets in 35 minutes from Cradley Heath! Gladys was so right. I soon got the measure of the 244, and when I learned how to keep on top of the job the route lost its terrors and was quite exhilarating.

'Cradley Heath garage was often used as the test-bed for experimental vehicles. The 'cattle truck' [the two-door standee 3919] put in an appearance working the 238/283 between Brickhouse Farm and Fatherless Barn estates.

This was an abject failure, but perhaps because it was used with a mobile conductor having to fight his way through a mob of standees. It might have worked with either a seated conductor or as one-man operation. I was nearly lumbered with this one Saturday, but happily the scheduled conductor turned up late and breathless, and I caught for a turn on the 243 instead.'

In the land of the Bard of Avon

'I established a good relationship for part-time work at Digbeth garage, and one afternoon, at my desk in the Timetables Office I got a call from them. Could I help them out with a late conducting turn on the 150 route between Birmingham and Stratford? When they told me the finishing time I knew I couldn't both pay in at Digbeth and get home on one of the last buses from town going back to Bearwood garage. So Bearwood agreed to sign me on, then "lend" me to Digbeth for the evening. So, at the end of the shift I could merely walk up, with all my gear, to High Street, catch my late bus, pay in at Bearwood, then walk home. Simple!

'Bearwood was now working with new Setright Speed model ticket machines but the poor Digbeth conductors were still scraping away with their Verometers. So, armed with waybill and Setright, I effected the relief at the Bull Ring terminus for our 7.15pm departure. Our first stop was opposite the garage, where a host of drivers and conductors, just finished their day's work, boarded to go home along the Stratford Road. They looked at me with some curiosity because firstly I was a complete stranger and secondly wore a "uniform" consisting only of a summer dustjacket topping a pair of plain grey flannels — clearly marking me out as a part-timer, or even a raw rookie.

'On the top deck the first passenger asked for nine tickets to Stratford. This would have involved much clattering and scraping and a veritable streamer of 18 tickets from a Verometer, and I saw some conductors turn round and positively leer at me. You could hear them thinking: "This is going to be fun." With a quick twist of the relevant dials I set the fare then, tucking a finger of one hand under the Setright to release the catch, with the other hand I wound the handle as fast as I could. Hey presto! Nine complete tickets to Stratford-on-Avon in quicker time than it took you to read this and their leers turned to gawps.

'I was at a loose end one Easter Monday so I ambled into Bearwood garage in case they might have a bit of work for a conductor. There was nothing doing, but Digbeth had rung up to say that there were big problems in clearing the Bank Holiday crowds from Stratford. With me, Bearwood had a conductor and were expecting a couple of buses to return any minute off Uttoxeter Races. As the two drivers handed in their waybills, the Inspector asked if either wished to do a Stratford. Unexpectedly they both, in unison, said yes. To save any argument I said that I could work both buses.

'Every September the anniversary of the Battle of Britain was celebrated by an Open Day at RAF Gaydon, on the A41 between Warwick and Banbury. A month later, there was the annual Warwick Mop Fair. Both of these events required lots of extra buses to cater for the great crowds that, in those days, used public transport. As these events took place on Saturdays, Leamington garage had plenty of buses to spare, but they hadn't the crews to man them.

'Enter Bearwood Head Office. A goodly gang culled from the clerical staff (suitably licensed, of course) made up a merry party of equal numbers of drivers and conductors to descend upon Leamington garage. Here each driver would be given a bus, and each conductor a ticket machine, waybill and running card — blank because our instructions were simply to "go out there and carry 'em".'

Above: Stan recalls that the local services radiating from Acocks Green were not the most popular at Digbeth. A nice conductress was considerable compensation, however, for a tired driver. *G. H. Stone*

Mop Fair

Historically an autumn fair at which farmhands and servants were hired. Each would carry an emblem of their trade, the name coming from the mop carried by maid-servants.

'One year, however, the Mop Fairs at Warwick and Stratford co-incided on the same day. My driver Bernard and I had been given an S13 for our day's work. We let the other crews disappear from Leamington on the L44 to Warwick, then, with a sly wink at Bernard I put up "518 Stratford" on the blind and we set off. This took us through Warwick, so we pulled our weight between the two towns, then on we toddled, through Barford and Wellesbourne, to Stratford, our bus getting more and more heavy-laden with "Stratford Moppers" as we progressed. On arrival in Stratford we were seized gladly by the duty inspector who made sure that we were kept busy.

'It was the monstrous queue for the 3.35pm 524 service to Evesham which caused us to be asked to run in front of

Suggestions for using your Anywhere Ticket

Based on the Summer Period—Saturday, 28th May, to Friday, 30th September, 1960

examples given in this Booklet are illustrative of journeys
h can be made in one day by 'Anywhere Ticket'. Many
r trips and variations of the ones shown can be made.
s have been given for the convenience of passengers, but
ny cases where frequent services are available, journeys
made earlier or later as desired, and our Enquiry Office
will be very pleased to work out details on application.
a ticket to freedom on Midland 'Red' buses, covering
inary services and enabling the holder to break his or her
at will—'Anywhere'.
ET MAY BE PURCHASED AT ANY MIDLAND 'RED' OFFICE AND MOST
(see list at end of booklet). IT CANNOT BE PURCHASED FROM CONDUCTORS.

R SPECIAL HOLIDAY SERVICES
LEASE SEE DETAILS AVAILABLE
OM ALL ENQUIRY OFFICES

Service No.	ROUTE	Time	Days	Single Fare
509	BANBURY (Town Hall) / COVENTRY (Pool Meadow)	10.35 a.m. / 11.56 a.m.	Saturdays / Saturdays	3/9
159	COVENTRY (Pool Meadow) / BIRMINGHAM (Bull Ring)	12.30 p.m. / 1.28 p.m.	Saturdays	2/4
148	BIRMINGHAM (Dudley Street) / EVESHAM (High Street)	1.45 p.m. / 3.39 p.m.	Saturdays	4/1
524	EVESHAM (High Street) / CHIPPING CAMPDEN	4.55 p.m. / 5.36 p.m.	Saturdays	1/8
496	CHIPPING CAMPDEN / BANBURY (Town Hall)	7. 3 p.m. / 8.23 p.m.	Saturdays	3/3
			TOTAL FARES	**15/1**

Service No.	ROUTE	Time	Days	Single Fare
509	BANBURY (Town Hall) / COVENTRY (Pool Meadow)	11.35 a.m. / 12.56 p.m.	Sunday / Sunday	3/9
517	COVENTRY (Pool Meadow) / LEAMINGTON (High Street)	2.25 p.m. / 3.4 p.m.	Sunday	1/8
571	LEAMINGTON (Althorpe Street) / RUGBY (Central Hotel)	5.10 p.m. / 6.8 p.m.	Sunday	2/3
X96	RUGBY (Central Hotel) / NORTHAMPTON (Mayor Hold)	7.12 p.m. / 8.10 p.m.	Sunday	2/8
512	NORTHAMPTON (Mayor Hold) / BANBURY (Town Hall)	8.10 p.m. / 9.40 p.m.	Sunday	3/7
			TOTAL FARES	**13/11**

Service No.	ROUTE	Friday	Sunday	Single Fare
480	BANBURY (Town Hall) / STRATFORD-ON-AVON (Red Lion)	9.10 a.m.† / 11.1 a.m.	2.30 p.m. / 4.3 p.m.	3/8
518	STRATFORD-ON-AVON (Red Lion) / WARWICK (Market Place)	12.35 p.m. / 1.13 p.m.	5.35 p.m. / 6.13 p.m.	1/8
L43	WARWICK (Market Place) / LEAMINGTON (High Street)	2.30 p.m. / 2.48 p.m.	7.0 p.m. / 7.18 p.m.	5½d.
517	LEAMINGTON (High Street) / COVENTRY (Pool Meadow)	3.30 p.m. / 4.9 p.m.	8.10 p.m. / 8.49 p.m.	1/8
509	COVENTRY (Pool Meadow) / BANBURY (Town Hall)	4.50 p.m. / 6.11 p.m.	9.5 p.m. / 10.26 p.m.	3/9
† Service 481			**TOTAL FARES**	**11/2½**

Service No.	ROUTE	Friday	Sunday	Single Fare
480	BANBURY (Town Hall) / STRATFORD-ON-AVON (Red Lion)	9.10 a.m.* / 11.1 a.m.	2.30 p.m. / 4.3 p.m.	3/8
150	STRATFORD-ON-AVON (Red Lion) / BIRMINGHAM (Bull Ring)	11.31 a.m. / 12.43 p.m.	4.31 p.m. / 5.43 p.m.	3/0
159	BIRMINGHAM (Bull Ring) / COVENTRY (Pool Meadow)	3.0 p.m. / 3.58 p.m.	7.0 p.m. / 7.58 p.m.	2/4
509	COVENTRY (Pool Meadow) / BANBURY (Town Hall)	4.50 p.m. / 6.11 p.m.	9.5 p.m. / 10.26 p.m.	3/9
* Service 481			**TOTAL FARES**	**12/9**

ROUTE	Time	Days	Single Fare
...RY (Town Hall) / ...NG CAMPDEN	8.0 a.m. / 9.32 a.m.	Saturdays / Saturdays	3/3
...NG CAMPDEN / ...RD-UPON-AVON (Bus Stn.)	10.36 a.m. / 11.17 a.m.	Saturdays / Saturdays	1/6
...RD-UPON-AVON (Bus Stn.) / ...TON SPA (High Street)	2.35 p.m. / 3.31 p.m.	Saturdays / Saturdays	1/10
...TON SPA (High Street) / ...Y (Pool Meadow)	6.15 p.m. / 6.54 p.m.	Saturdays / Saturdays	1/8
...Y (Pool Meadow) / ...(Town Hall)	7.5 p.m. / 8.26 p.m.	Saturdays / Saturdays	3/9
		TOTAL FARES	**12/0**

ROUTE	Time	Days	Single Fare
...own Hall) / ...TON (Mayor Hold)	9.10 a.m. / 10.40 a.m.	Saturdays / Saturdays	3/7
...ON (Mayor Hold) / ...(Bull Ring)	12.45 p.m. / 3.32 p.m.	Saturdays / Saturdays	5/8
...(Bull Ring) / ...SPA (High Street)	4.30 p.m. / 5.58 p.m.	Saturdays / Saturdays	3/0
...SPA (High Street) / ...(Pool Meadow)	6.15 p.m. / 6.54 p.m.	Saturdays / Saturdays	1/8
COVENTRY (Pool Meadow) / BANBURY (Town Hall)	7.5 p.m. / 8.26 p.m.	Saturdays / Saturdays	3/9
		TOTAL FARES	**17/8**

Day Anywhere tickets for Midland Red's stage-carriage services were reintroduced in 1958. The company encouraged people to travel as many miles as possible in one day — a challenge particularly taken up by bus enthusiasts. The X44 Birmingham–Worcester motorway service would prove a valuable way of clocking up miles after 1962, so Midland Red laid down a rule to the highest-mileage claimants that this could be used only once!

Stratford Blue inspector had to ride on the step holding the pushchair. For me, as conductor, I had to enter by the rear emergency door to collect the fares.

'Then the queue for the 8 o'clock 150 to Birmingham was reaching unmanageable proportions, so into the breach we stepped. It was an irony to set down all our passengers in Birmingham's Bull Ring just after 9 o'clock, knowing that we were so near home, yet we had to get bus, ticket machine (and money!) all back to Leamington before we could think of reaching our homes so tantalisingly nearby.

A touch of the blues

'One Saturday there was a gala being held on a firm's sports field between Monkspath and Solihull, on the very busy 154 route. An extra bus would be needed to ferry the expected crowds. Digbeth had neither the bus nor the crew to manage it. Bearwood had me as a conductor and a phone call to Don Everall quickly got us a bus and driver. Off we set to the Bull Ring to help out on the 154.

'You can imagine the consternation when this bus drew up at Midland Red stops *en route* because it was painted blue and cream! It was a Daimler utility, still in the colours of its former owner, Sheffield Corporation. We got round

it to Lower Quinton. No problem here — a simple run along what was then the main A46. By the time we reached Lower Quinton turn we had just a handful of folk left on from the full standing load with which we had left Stratford. "You turn left here into the village to turn round," said the last passenger to get off. So off we trundled, looking for a suitable turning-place. Unfortunately we must have missed something vital. Have you ever tried a 14-point turn with an S13, in gathering gloom, in a farmyard into which the lane had petered out? Yes, I got lost in Quinton — but not the one I live in!

'Getting back to Stratford we did a bit more shuttling to places like Tiddington. One such trip we had so many passengers that when a young couple tried to board with a pushchair we squeezed them on somehow, but a

Right: There were interesting developments at Leicester, where several significant businesses were acquired from the mid-1950s. One was Allen's of Mountsorrel, with effect from 30 July 1955. No Allen vehicles were added to stock, but the company had a subsidiary, Kemp & Shaw, whose buses were retained in their original livery until 1959, when the eight survivors were numbered 4838-45 and painted in Midland Red colours. Included among these were two 1949 Guy Arab IIIs with Gardner 5LW engines and 35-seat Barnard bodies, reintroducing vertical-engined single-deckers to the fleet. They lasted until 1962, straying from Leicester to operate from Shrewsbury, Ludlow, Lichfield and Coalville. *Omnicolour*

the problem for the duration of the gala by shuttling between Blossomfield and Shirley, thus avoiding clashing with other blue and cream buses inside the city boundary. And at least we held our own with Sheepcote Street's red-painted versions of the same marque.'

A foggy phenomenon

'I was having a quiet December morning on the Saturday morning shift in the Timetables Office at Bearwood. Digbeth called and asked if I was free for a late conducting duty. Gosh! A trip to Cheltenham on the X73, no less!

'I knew the road well, at least as far as Coombe Hill, where the X72 to Gloucester and the X73 to Cheltenham diverged. I travelled it every week for nearly two years on my weekend pass from RAF Innsworth. By the time we reached Bromsgrove night had fallen, but all went well until we reached Kempsey, the other side of Worcester. Here we met a most unusual weather freak. It was a beautiful starlit night, I could see for miles through the windscreen, yet my driver had to reduce speed to a crawl, so much so that we were twenty minutes late arriving in Cheltenham. The cause was fog that had spread over the ground from the River Severn nearby. It was no more than 3ft high, so while I could see for miles, my driver couldn't see the road! It was certainly odd.'

Dealing with the Union

'It will be self-evident that a Scheduler's work directly affects the working conditions of platform staff. Therefore one cannot avoid coming into contact with the Trade Union in the case of Midland Red, the T&GWU.

'In the eyes of many the unions were the "baddies", but this would be totally misleading when referring to the Union representatives I had to deal with. My earliest brush with a union official was at a meeting with the Bearwood Garage union committee.

'The chairman in those days was the company's senior driver for the Birmingham area. He was always allocated the prestige jobs — if royalty, say, was to be carried on a Midland Red vehicle he would be the driver. One cannot deny his skill as a driver, as he was the one who successfully brought a CM5T coach to a smooth stand after an 85mph blow-out in the opening parade of the M1 motorway. During the summer months he was always away driving the company's prestigious Scottish cruises.

'He was back "in-house" when this meeting was held in the winter, so rather lorded it over the meeting. Something I said prompted him to look scornfully down his nose at me. "You people sit so comfortably at your desks upstairs and really haven't an idea what it's like on the road." And he went on at me in the same vein, the Superintendent looking on somewhat uncomfortably.

'As the chairman paused for effect one of the drivers present spoke up. "Excuse me, Harry, but I think you should know that Mr Letts was my mate on the late 252 last night, and he ain't a bad conductor."

'To give Harry his due, he was a gentleman. He paused, looked straight at me and said: "It appears I owe you an apology." From then on that meeting — and all subsequent ones —were conducted quite cordially.'

Bright ideas encouraged

'It should not be assumed that a Scheduler was woken from seasonal slumber only when new services had to be scheduled. On the contrary, problems large and small would crop up most days, but there were some slack times. It was during such moments that I succumbed to brain-waves. It speaks volumes for the enlightened Midland Red management that they actively encouraged such creative thoughts and initiatives.

'One of my thoughts was aimed at the company's route map. Although it was nicely produced in several colours, the size of paper on which the whole of the operating territory was shown (some 100 miles in diameter) meant that fine detail was impossible. Like Midland Red, Western and Southern National timetable books were issued in separate

Left: One of two Leyland Titan PD2s acquired with Kemp & Shaw had Leyland's own bodywork to 'lowbridge' side-gangway configuration, the only such vehicle to operate in the Midland Red fleet. GRY 763 was numbered 4844; despite its inconvenient interior layout it ran for many years, until 1967, by which time it was 17 years old. This is St Margaret's bus station in November 1961. *Maurice Collignon*

Right: Both Kemp & Shaw PD2s were fitted with Midland Red destination displays before full absorption into the fleet in 1959. Seen in August 1958, the future 4845, a PD2/12 dating from 1952, was effectively an exposed-radiator version of the LD8. Alongside is a Trent Willowbrook-bodied AEC Regent II, mechanically similar to the AD2s. *Richard Butler*

Left: H. Boyer & Son of Rothley remained the only independent on the Leicester–Mountsorrel road after Kemp & Shaw fell to Midland Red. Only one more week and this Boyer crew would be employees of Midland Red, the company being taken over on 1 February 1959. Three single-deckers were added to BMMO stock as 4846-8. Two were particularly surprising, being comparatively rare 1951 Sentinels, of which this one became 4846. Sentinel, based in Shrewsbury, had introduced underfloor-engined single-deckers shortly after BMMO and before the major manufacturers. *Richard Butler*

Right: Saturday 31 January 1959 — the last day of Boyer. HJU 546, about to become BMMO 4848, loads at Rothley Green. This Leyland Royal Tiger, with Leyland's own 44-seat bodywork, had been new in 1952 to Allen of Mountsorrel and in 1966 would be sold to Stevensons of Uttoxeter for several more years' service. The final significant Leicester-area purchase was Brown's Blue Coaches Ltd, in 1963. No vehicles were taken over, but the Brown's Blue garage at Markfield was used by Midland Red for five years.
Richard Butler

areas. Each area book contained a skeletal map of the whole territory on one side, while the reverse side showed a superbly detailed map, with service numbers etc, for that book's area.

'I thought that Midland Red could do likewise and did a test map of one of the areas. The management liked the idea, which was then applied to all of the company's different timetable books. I did all the work myself in spare moments and lots of (unpaid!) overtime, carefully tracing the route of every service onto huge sheets of paper.'

Anywhere goes!

'The other rather interesting self-appointed task was when the company revived Day Anywhere Tickets. I was the one who, every spring, used actual timetables for compiling the booklet suggesting day trips by bus from various locations, and covering the most popular beauty spots and scenic rides.

'Our responsibilities also included the task of supplying printers with handwritten copy for the production of public timetable leaflets for every service. Woe betide any scheduler who failed to get a revised leaflet out to the public at least seven days before its introduction. Not only timetable leaflets but also we had to ensure that outside garages were promptly furnished with the new timetable posters for display along the routes. Changes also had to be entered into the "master dummies" of the area timetable books so that they would be correct when they went for their twice-yearly printing.

'Unlike today's deregulated regimen, every change to a timetable or line of route had to be approved by the Traffic Commissioners. It was the Scheduler's task to prepare the requisite documentation seeking to vary the licence for that service (and giving reasons for the change). There were bodies that could object to an application, and when this occurred there would be a hearing at the Area Traffic Court. Usually the case was presented to the court by a company Licensing Officer specialising in Traffic Court proceedings, with sometimes the Scheduler being present at the hearing in case he was required to enter the witness box to give supporting evidence.'

Good relations

'Because I kept them well supplied with up-to-date time-table leaflets, I had a very friendly working relationship with the ladies of Bearwood enquiry office. One of them eventually decided to leave and, to prove how small the world is, her name was Mary Mills — sister of the eminent Bob.

'Her replacement was transferred from the Engineers' typing pool. The "Nut & Bolt Department" was out of my usual ken, so the new girl, Marie, came as a complete stranger. She herself, however, was no stranger to the bus industry, as her father worked for the neighbouring Gliderways Coaches, and was a former Devon General driver.

'We got on well with each other. Very well indeed! I married her and Marie was to be my companion for just over forty years (until cancer took her) during which I looked at no other.'

The Friendly Midland Red

The company had evidently kept a ciné-camera for its own use for some time. However, in the mid-1950s, it decided to produce its own promotional films. The first effort, around 45 minutes long, promoted Scottish tours. Fortunately the company's strong social side had given rise to the Midland 'Red' Symphony Orchestra and the Midland 'Red' Male Voice Choir which had evolved by this time into the Midland 'Red' Salon Orchestra and Singers.

Mr L. F. P. Trueman, Publicity Superintendent, and Mr Leslie Riley, Deputy Coach Cruise Superintendent, undertook the shooting of the film, apart from some footage taken previously by Traffic Manager Richard Brandon. Handily Mr Riley was also Musical Director of the Orchestra and composed the music. Mr Trueman wrote the commentary, spoken by Mr Riley, so everything including editing was achieved in-house, apart from the initial processing of the film. The film was shown across the Midlands to encourage coach cruise patronage. Many more were to follow, including one promoting stage carriage services after the reintroduction of Day Anywhere tickets.

12 | Working the X99

The X99 (Birmingham–Nottingham) was a typical route for Midland Red's dual-purpose buses, of which the S13s were the first. **Phil Crook**'s father, Charlie, was a driver at Tamworth, including before the S13s when the best of the single-deckers would be used. Phil himself was a Tamworth conductor for some years and shares some family memories of the X99.

'I had been a keen Midland Red enthusiast since around age five, probably because my father was a driver at Tamworth. Just postwar, my father was on Notts one Sunday, and I was "invited" to come on the Tamworth–Nottingham leg, 5.20pm ex Tamworth. The X99 at that time left from Aldergate, outside Coates' shop, the then parcel agents. I counted five extras in front. I recall Dad was at the back, and he was driving a GHA SON, which were favourites on the X99 at that time, until the arrival of the S6s. I remember the return trip, being stuck in many Army convoys, but we were on time when I left him at Tamworth.

'My father had brake failure on an X99 inbound to Birmingham with 3912, I think, whilst descending Gravelly Hill, near to Kingsbury Road. This occurred in 1953 just before the Salford Bridge group of trams were withdrawn. A route 2 tram was stationary, and the tram conductor stood open-mouthed as my father was flashing lights and blowing the horn, while his guard shouted at the top of

his voice, to get the tram to move. Fortunately no one was injured, but the tram crew were severely told off by the guard, and the tram driver requested to wake up his dozy conductor!

'I started as a conductor at Tamworth in the mid-1950s, just before the growth of daily car travel. Tamworth, until the 1960s, was a small market town; the main employments in the area were coal mining, agriculture, the clay works, and the Reliant car factory. When I started conducting I was familiar with all of the local routes, and knew most of the fare stages. I did a week's training at the conductors' school at Sheepcote Street, which of course I found easy as I had understood time- and fare tables ever since I could read (!) and the recently introduced Setright ticket machine was a big improvement on previous methods of fare collection.

'On typical summer Saturday and Sunday shifts, especially Bank Holidays, most X99 buses had duplicates. I have worked on the service bus ex Nottingham, picking up a Coalville extra at Ashby, and a Swadlincote bus at Measham. Sometimes they would meet us in Nottingham and work through to Birmingham. Bank Holiday times would also see a Sutton bus inwards to the city and we would be joined by a Digbeth bus for the return to Nottingham. Not much room at either end for us, let alone Trent!

'I have been on the service bus and had duplicates from Tamworth, Coalville, Swadlincote, Sutton and Digbeth. The usual formation would be the Tamworth or Coalville bus in the lead, as we 'knew the road' with the duplicate behind. It was also known to swap guards, ie one of us go with (say) the Digbeth driver to help show the road, but this was very much frowned upon, as the wrong revenue went to the wrong shed.

'We used to deliver lots of parcels on the Midland Red network. One day I returned to my bus in Station Street, Birmingham, to find the parcels boy from Dudley Street busy loading the first two rows of seats on either side with very large boxes of needles. This was a usual occurrence, as they would be sent from Redditch to Alfreton via Midland Red and Trent. This of course deprived me of eight seats from a total of 40, usually no problem as Suttonites seemed to love the status of riding on X services, and were only short distance riders. We arrived at Wylde Green Post Office and stopped for intending passengers, when two ladies appeared with a large pram and attempted to board the bus. I asked them their intended destination as I had limited space and fitting large pushchairs on an S15 was almost impossible. They said that they wanted to go to Sutton. I pointed out that there was no room on my bus, but a 103-route double-decker was just behind. Problem sorted, but my driver was Biggles who fancied himself as a fighter pilot. He had to interfere, saying that if it were up to him they could have boarded, and he was still moaning about it at Sutton.

'About a week later I had the proverbial "brown envelope". This meant that a complaint had been received against me, and I was to see the Area Disciplinary Officer. I waited for one of the union committee drivers to finish his shift — no full-time union officials then. I was lucky, I had the garage chairman who would represent me at the hearing. We went to see the Traffic Superintendent. We read the letter which, if it hadn't meant my possible dismissal, would have been laughable. The gist was that I refused to pick up passengers, told them to walk and similar statements, and that the driver had pleaded with me to let them on board. The union rep asked who the driver was. When I replied Biggles, he said not to worry too much and leave the talking to him.

'When we went into the disciplinary office, the charge against me was read out and I was asked what I had to say for myself. I said that my union rep would speak for me. He asked the disciplinary officer to note the name of the driver, the destination of the women, the frequency of buses on that road to Sutton and also the amount of parcels I was carrying. Within minutes the case was dismissed.

'The X99 timetables used to show a connection (not guaranteed) with Trent seaside destinations, especially Skegness, in the summer. Driver Billy Williamson was late taking over one summer's day; traffic in Birmingham had delayed the bus. At Ashby, an elderly couple approached Bill and asked if he could make up any time, as they wanted to catch the Skegness connection. Bill said that he would do his best but, just past the bends in Isley Walton, the bus was stopped for speeding. The gentleman intervened and told the policeman that the X99 was late and that he wanted to catch the Skegness coach. The police agreed, and Billy drew into Mount Street just before the coach was due to leave. The grateful passengers gave Billy five shillings, which was a reasonable sum at that time.'

Above: Tamworth's enquiry office, with the usual postwar black fascia relieved by the wheel-and-tyre motif in colour. This style was looking distinctly funereal by 1968, the date of this picture, contrasting with the jolly advertising on view. *BMMO*

Not always sunny weather

'It would be in the winter of 1960/1 that I was scheduled to take over the 12.20 departure from Tamworth to Nottingham with driver Ken Terry, a former Nottingham man. We were due to take over an S14, but for some reason this had to be taken off the road, so we were given S12 3743, a rarity for Notts — usually S13s or S15s were used with S14s as reserve. The weather was fairly snowy, but nothing was sticking to the roads, so there was no reason to expect any delays. The journey to Nottingham was reasonable, and good timing was kept on the way back until we reached Newton Regis crossroads, where we were stopped by the police, as an accident between two cars had occurred. They had apparently both skidded on the snow, and blocked the road to Tamworth. After some discussion between the police and myself, Ken decided to attempt to turn toward Newton village then head through Seckington village and along a lane to rejoin the A453 to Tamworth. I knew the road very well, and the police confirmed that the lanes were not blocked. We came through Newton and Seckington, but the lane up to the main road was covered with some small drifts. During snowy weather we were supposed to obtain a shovel from the engineers to move snow from under the rear wheels, or to spread salt or gravel under the wheels. I had to use the shovel a couple of times, but we managed to reach the A453 without too much trouble. Ken then said that he would not have attempted that route with an S14, as the rear wheels were single and had no tyre grip in the snow.'

13 | The final flowering of BMMO

With the combined problems of ever-worsening staff shortage, rising costs and poor patronage of many rural services, the company began to introduce one-man-operated S14s; the first at Hereford in 1956. Some S14s entered service as such and most were later converted. The bus industry was notoriously poorly paid and recruitment on both platform and engineering sides became steadily more difficult. There were better-paid jobs in manufacturing industries, and bus companies were particularly disadvantaged with platform staff because there was not the opportunity to recruit new personnel straight from school. It was not legally possible to employ someone as a conductor until the age of 18; similarly you could not progress onwards to a driver until you were 21. The company did employ youths in various capacities such as parcel messengers, finding them other work at the age of 18, including the opportunity to become conductors. This would only meet a fraction of the company's conducting needs, however. A slight help in the 1950s had been compulsory National Service in one of the armed forces. Some young men let their careers drift in dead-end jobs until National Service was completed and then looked for career posts afterwards. The end of National Service removed this opportunity to recruit young men at the outset of their careers as platform staff.

As the 1960s approached, the company produced several final flourishes of technological brilliance before the long night of decline rapidly set in.

Left: 'What did you do at work today, dear?' 'Going around in circles' would have been the answer as test drivers sped round MIRA's speed track at Lindley, near Nuneaton. BMMO tested the new CM5T coaches for months before the M1 opened, because these were to be the country's first motorway-express coaches and, in technological terms, represented uncharted waters — no British coach had hitherto been asked to cruise at speeds anything like 80mph. Midland Red had them on the road from the very first day and gained national prestige. They were soon fitted with twin headlights. *BMMO*

Right: The CM5T interior was considered quite racy in its time. *The Transport Museum, Wythall*

Left: High-speed running brought levels of sprayed dirt never previously seen! One dreads to think of the state of the roads to generate the amount of salt caked on 4814, on the patch behind Digbeth coach station after a round trip to London. Wooden route boards above the windows of the motorway coaches were a delightful yet antiquated feature. A motorway version without toilet, the CM5, was introduced for the X44 Birmingham–Worcester service, introduced on 20 July 1962, opening day of the new M5 motorway. Nos 4833-5 were allocated to Worcester and 4836/7 to Digbeth for the new service. *R. Mallabon / The Transport Museum, Wythall*

The fastest coaches in Britain

The last scheduled S14 was actually built as the prototype of a new generation of chassisless coaches of completely new design. This was C5 4722 of 1958, and construction of the 64-strong production batch began the next year. Their 'lantern'-style windscreens gave them a particularly distinctive appearance but the real moment of glory came when motorway variants entered service on the opening day of the M1, Britain's first proper motorway, on 2 November 1959.

The modified design was styled CM5T, the additional letters standing for 'Motorway' and 'Toilet', the latter until then rare on British coaches, comfort breaks previously being the norm. The toilet compartment reduced the seating capacity from 37 to 34. Many C5s were initially fitted with four-speed gearboxes. All were later fitted with five-speed boxes but these were employed on the CM5T from new. Other important changes on the CM5T were a turbocharged version of the KL engine, a modified rear axle ratio and larger front tyres.

Right: More sub-classes were evolved within the 64 production C5 vehicles. The C5A designation was applied to any variant demoted to bus services and fitted with an inward-opening entrance door and modified destination box. Their numbers swelled after larger coaches were introduced on motorway services to replace the CM5Ts, which additionally had their turbochargers removed. They still looked fine thanks to their handsome straight lines. Leamington's 4783 loads at Pool Meadow, Coventry, on 27 April 1968. *Patrick Kingston*

Left: The CS5 variant remained primarily for normal coach duties but, although not turbocharged, could be used as a duplicate or emergency replacement on high-speed motorway services. Climbing Green Bank on the Stratford Road in Hall Green, Birmingham, on 6 June 1969, 4784 has the maroon roof introduced to replace black on repaints from May 1967; note, however, that the centre of the roof is a lighter colour, to reflect heat. Regrettably even coaches would lose any relief colour from November 1970. *Malcolm Keeley*

'The Bus Driver's Dream of Home'

This was how a trade-press writer described the BMMO D9. As far back as 1951 Midland Red was interested in developing a 30ft-long double-decker. Drawings dating from that time show features that were to be typical of the D9, but double-deckers of that length were not legal until 1956. By that time BMMO was interested in integral vehicles with disc brakes and rubber suspension so, when the D9 was unveiled in 1958, it was by no means an extended D7. Instead 4773 was a remarkably advanced chassisless 72-seater. Amongst the features was the new 10.5-litre engine, coupled to a semi-automatic gearbox; the driver also benefited from power steering.

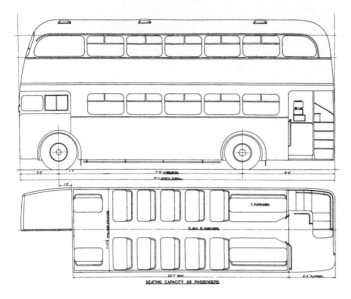

Left: Gestation of the D9. The 1951 Metro-Cammell drawing reveals BMMO's hopes that double-deckers would soon fall in line with the recent increase in maximum length to 30ft for single-deckers. At that time maximum weight restrictions would have been a cause of concern for designers, so perhaps platform doors were omitted to keep weight down. Already in mind is the D9's classic set-back front axle, necessitating inward-facing seats but giving advantages in terms of a shorter wheelbase (and hence a reduced turning-circle), improved engine access and a reduction in weight on the rear axle. Another drawing shows a Bristol Lodekka-style arrangement with rearward-facing seats across the front bulkhead, allowing one extra seat.

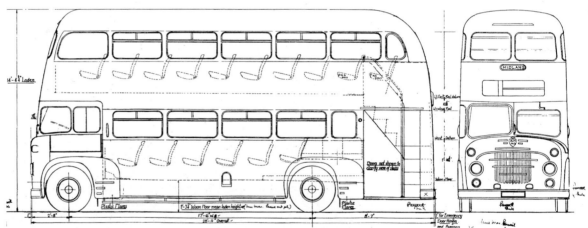

Above: Future permitted length was uncertain; this BMMO design was to an intermediate length of 29ft, seating 67; another drawing of the same date shows a 30-footer seating 73. Note that on this drawing the axle is in the orthodox position. The coach-style mudwings are also impressive!

Right: Prototype D9 4773 gleams at Central Works in 1958. Providing a contrast is D5B 3869, while just visible in between is S14 4710. *The Transport Museum, Wythall*

Production D9s began appearing in 1960, and had a number of detail body improvements. The disc brake did not prove itself in the double-decker application (mainly because of excessive pad wear) and early production vehicles had these brakes on the front wheels only. The system remained unsuccessful and later D9s were fitted with drum brakes all round — the earlier vehicles were modified accordingly. Braking then became one of the D9's worst features!

Below: A 1960 view of the Production Shop full of D9s under construction, along with a C5 on the extreme right. *BMMO*

Left: Mr D. M. Sinclair CBE, M I Mech E, M Inst T (right) looks ready to comment that the conversion to metric measurements had not gone well. In fact the gentleman on the left is Mr Joseph Faulkner, a body-maker at Central Works, handing over his last model, a D9, upon his retirement after 36 years with BMMO. Mr Faulkner produced superb scale models of the company's buses dating back to horse-bus days. Normally these graced Mr Sinclair's office, but one was often in a display window at the Bearwood offices. They were also exhibited at home and abroad, promoting the company's activities. Happily the models still exist. *BMMO*

Right: Tally ho! Production D9 5354 races away from Burges, Coventry, outpacing a pair of Corporation Daimlers — Fleetline/ECW 25 and CVG6/Metro-Cammell 303. The date is June 1972, and 5354 carries a later style of fleet-name. No fewer than 345 D9s were produced, and, in the best BMMO tradition, changes were numerous. A significant one for passengers was the introduction, from bus 4988, of fluorescent lighting, following trial installations on 4927 and 4949. *The Transport Museum, Wythall*

Underfloor-engined double-deckers

Hardly had the dust settled after the launch of the D9 prototype than the trade press announced, in November 1958, that similar running units would be featured in a BMMO double-decker with underfloor engine. The article, accompanied by drawings, described the future D10 almost exactly as it would subsequently appear. BMMO technical expertise reached its peak when the completed D10 prototype, bus 4943, was revealed in September 1960. BMMO astounded manufacturers that had felt underfloor-engine double-deckers were not practicable as the floor level would be too high to allow a double-deck body.

The D10 had been a long time in gestation. The July 1949 *Staff Bulletin* recorded that: *'The question of producing an underfloor-engined double-decker is engaging the Company's attention at the present time; but the problem is not easily solved, principally because of overall height'.* To avoid raising the floor level, BMMO placed the engine the opposite way round to that in single-deckers, *i.e.* with cylinder heads towards the centre and the crankcase towards the nearside. The deepest part of the engine, the flywheel housing, was thus outside the area restricted by legal minimum-ground-clearance regulations and clear of the lower-saloon gangway.

No 4943 was capable of holding 80 passengers, but a near straight staircase, giving exceptional ease of use and generous luggage accommodation beneath, reduced capacity to 78. Drawings for a whole family of D10-based vehicles exist, including rear-entrance, two-door (front and rear), low-bridge, and single-deck versions. The D10 was not unsuccessful but its advantage over the simpler D9 for one-man operation was not foreseen at the time. Only one more D10 was built. Bus 4944 of 1961 trialled the two-door, twin-staircase arrangement, seating only 65. It was rebuilt to single-door and -staircase in November 1962.

Left: The integral D10s were built at Central Works using the established steel bodyframe to BMMO design, manufactured by Metal Sections Ltd, which had been the supplier since the S14. Metalastik, as usual, supplied the rubber suspension. Dual-door 4944 was styled the D10 MkII. Seen here at Dudley while working from Hartshill garage, it received rather muted coverage in the *Staff Bulletin*, perhaps indicating that there were doubts from the outset about its layout. *The Transport Museum, Wythall*

Right: The D10 radiator was positioned at the front (without a cooling fan). Locating the engine and transmission within the 16ft 9in wheelbase resulted in a remarkably stable vehicle. This is 4944 after rebuilding with single door and staircase. *MRK collection*

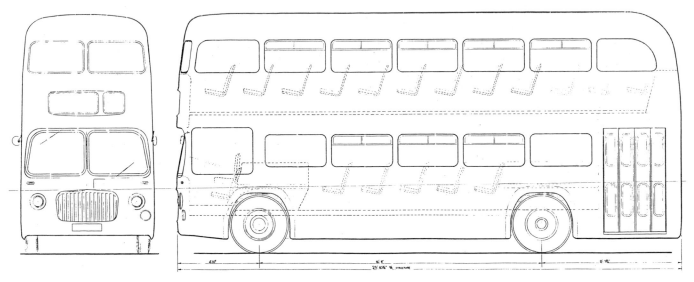

Above: August 1958 drawing of a rear-entrance D10, permitting up to 82 seats, including a highly desirable pair alongside the driver.

Below: A 73-seat lowbridge D10 with, behind the staircase, sunken upper-deck gangway. This is intriguing, as Midland Red had no need of lowbridge buses.

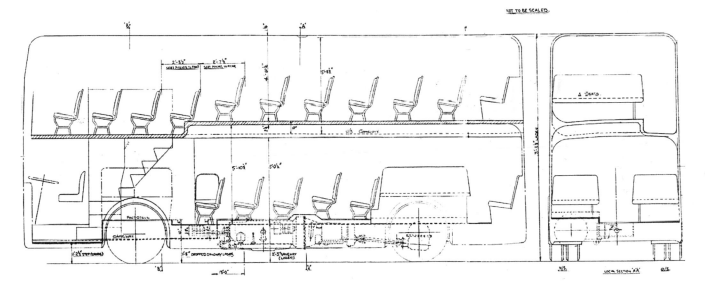

Below: D10-based 36ft-long single-decker with 50 seats, drawn 13 February 1961, six months before buses of this length were permitted. The design would have permitted a much lower saloon height compared with the standard S models.

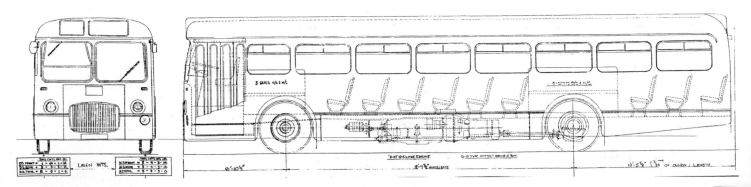

14 | Descending the downward staircase

So ended the golden days. There was one more brief moment of glory, however. Midland Red services out of Birmingham departed from streets scattered over the city centre — highly unsatisfactory for those changing from one route to another. This ended in November 1963 when a new bus station opened, adjacent to the Bull Ring Centre. This was used by all Midland Red bus services except the Dudley Road services jointly run with Birmingham City Transport, and long-distance coach services which continued to use Digbeth coach station. The new bus station was entirely undercover and gave staff proper canteen and toilet facilities but, in time, generated justified passenger complaints about fumes.

The first vehicles to the newly permitted dimensions of 36ft length and 8ft 2in width were the 52-seat S16 buses, built in 1962/3. They were stretched versions of the S14/S15 with too many side windows and lacklustre performance, retaining the 8-litre engine and constant-

Left: In 1960 bus 3220 was extended to a length of 45ft, to play its part in convincing the Ministry that longer single-deckers were feasible. Here it is at Central Works, with the rear extension not yet clothed. It reverted to normal in 1961; new legal maximum dimensions were sanctioned for coaches and single-decker buses from 1 August of that year, permitting a length of 36ft and width of 8ft 2½in. *G. H. Stone*

Right: Hired buses and drivers, with Midland Red conductors, were employed for many years from Leamington and the practice spread in the 1960s. This G&G Coaches driver, with the splendid ex-Devon General 1946 RT-type AEC Regent III bodied by Weymann, was having a Midland Red working day without being an employee. *Alan D. Broughall*

Below: The 36-footers increased the efficiency of the crews. The introduction of such buses to replace the ageing early-postwar fleet was accelerated in 1962/3 by the purchase of 100 Leyland Leopards with semi-automatic gear-boxes, the LS18 class. Twenty-five were bodied by Weymann, but most, including 5233 here, had Willowbrook bodies. Carrying a later lettering style, it was employed in March 1973 on one of Midland Red's more obscure local services — the K prefix representing not Kidderminster but Kenilworth, as the ludicrous destination display confirms! *Patrick Kingston*

Above: Midland Red quickly built a single-decker to the new permitted dimensions, prototype S16 5095 being licensed from April 1962. Further S14 buses had been intended, and the S16 was very much a stretched version, employing the same mechanical units. This in turn was followed by the S17, similar in appearance but with the bigger (10.5-litre) engine and semi-automatic gearbox. A valuable improvement, bearing in mind the increase in seating capacity to 52, was the wider entrance door. S17 5685 of 1965 pulls past preserved Birmingham Leyland PD2/Brush 1685 at the old entrance to Birmingham Airport, Elmdon, in June 1969. *Malcolm Keeley*

mesh gearbox. The S17 quickly followed and was much more popular with drivers enjoying the BMMO 10.5-litre engine and semi-automatic gearbox. Similar to the S17 was one S19 that principally differed with modified suspension. Drivers probably turned pale in 1964 when 34 further S16s were built. These used the four-speed constant-mesh gear-boxes removed from C5 coaches converted to five-speed. Three 1965 S17s, 5722-4, were built as dual-purpose, 48-seat vehicles and designated S21A. Each had different trim and upholstery to gain passenger reaction for future production. They were re-classified S22 in 1967 and S17 upon downgrading to bus status in 1971.

The success of Midland Red's high-speed motorway services soon prompted thoughts of coaches to the new, increased dimensions. A prototype 36ft-long coach, No 5295, entered service in March 1963, designated the CM6T. This incorporated the 10.5-litre engine with a manual five-speed gearbox, changed after about three months in service to two-pedal semi-automatic. In appearance it was effectively a lengthened CM5T; the styling was subsequently re-worked, and even more so on the 29 production

coaches built in 1965/6. Most notable were the wider pillar spacings — the first such change since 1946! Five did not have toilets, being intended for the Birmingham–Worcester express services, all others being the 44-seat CM6T variety for longer motorway duties.

The then healthy motor industry of the 1960s meant BMMO found it difficult to replace the old-timers as they retired, and many younger skilled engineers were tempted away. Increasing numbers of Leyland Leopards and Daimler Fleetlines had to be bought to supplement the falling output of new vehicles from Carlyle Works. By the mid-1960s a large number of BMMO vehicles had only the main body structure completed at Carlyle Works, finishing work being undertaken by Willowbrook or Plaxton.

Some garages experienced chronic shortages of engineering staff and reliability fell. A number of vehicles were hired with drivers, a costly manoeuvre to stem the loss of passengers forced away by unreliable services. The gradual spread of one-man operation, both as an economy measure and a way of increasing bus drivers' pay, reduced the staff problems slightly on the platform side. It was extended to double-deckers in 1968, using Daimler Fleetlines.

Mr Sinclair retired at the end of 1966, after a quarter of a century with the company, and was succeeded by his deputy, Mr. J. W. Womar, formerly General Manager of Potteries Motor Traction.

With Mr Sinclair gone and falling levels of BMMO production, those wishing to continue the breed found themselves outgunned. Dick Nutt had left Midland Red in the mid-1950s and met his former colleague Ray Braithwaite upon the retirement of their old boss, now

Chief Engineer, Jack Ransome. Mr Braithwaite had pursued a career moving around other bus companies in the British Electric Traction group, returning to Midland Red in the 1960s. He made the point to Dick that he could buy Leyland buses and coaches far cheaper than it cost the Midland Red to build its own, and the parlous state of the company meant economy had to take precedence over sentiment.

The final series of 143 BMMO-built buses were more 36-footers, mechanically almost identical to the S17s. The body structure, however, was based on the CM6

Right: C2s 3346/50/2 were rebodied with 26-seat Plaxton Embassy bodies. No 3352 is seen after repainting in red and black but retaining, for the time being, a cream band. Note that the rebodies had no provision for a destination blind. *The Transport Museum, Wythall*

Left: By 1962 the tour-coach fleet was looking jaded. Rather than designing a new model with only a small production run, BMMO had Scarborough coachbuilder Plaxton rebody three C2 and 16 C3 coaches, reclassified CL2 and CL3 respectively; another C3 was similarly treated in time for the 1964 season. The CL3s, seating 36, had Plaxton's recently introduced 'Panorama' body and looked right up-to-date with their big fixed windows and forced-air ventilation. They were, however, painted plain cream all over; this was very unpopular with regular tour clients, and they had to be repainted in the traditional red and black after one season. Sadly, 10 years later, NBC ignored the lesson. *Plaxton*

Right: The 65 coaches in the C5 family had replaced the 25 ONC coaches, but, such was the buoyancy of coach demand, hardly any C1s were withdrawn in the early 1960s, most lasting until 1965; this was a remarkable lifespan for coaches, and it was a credit to their designers that they so easily withstood the passage of time. Most of the early withdrawals were retained for other purposes: 3301 became the company's orchestra coach, while the driver-training fleet eventually included 3307/8/11/23/6/7/32/40/1; Nos 3327/41 were not finally sold until 1976. For a time driver-trainer 3311 was painted in the very attractive scheme used for coaches and dual-purpose buses built after 1958. In January 1968, when this photograph was taken, it was Leamington's training vehicle. Upon withdrawal it became an unusual choice of hospitality vehicle for Arnold Plant Sales, of Brierley Hill; nowadays it is preserved by Colin Hawketts. *Patrick Kingston*

production coaches, with wider pillar spacings and single rear window, with the emergency door moved to the offside. Three different interior finishes reflected the work the buses were intended to do. The last bus to be completed entirely at Carlyle was S23 5941, which left the Works on 5 January 1970 after a small ceremony. Plaxton completed the bodywork on the remaining vehicles with the last one, 5991, entering service in June 1970. All that knowledge and experience of vehicle design and building then went to waste.

Into state hands

The Great Western Railway and the London, Midland & Scottish Railway had purchased half the ordinary shares in BMMO in April 1930. 1 January 1948 saw the nationalisation of the railways by the Labour government, meaning that the railway companies' shareholdings became state-owned. British Electric Traction, owners of Midland Red, considered that nationalisation should be fought to the last ditch. Progress on bus nationalisation was thus slow and the 1951 General Election saw the Conservatives returned to power. Midland Red thus continued as a privately controlled company under BET with a proportion of its shares owned by the state.

Economic times for the bus industry began to get harder, however. Despite openly declared opposition by Midland Red to nationalisation, BET agreed in November 1967 to sell its shareholdings in UK bus operating companies to the state-owned Transport Holding Company. Thus, from 14 March 1968, Midland Red became wholly owned by the THC and, on 1 January 1969, a subsidiary of the new National Bus Company. The NBC believed in much more central control than BET, and the company lost much of its individuality. The succession of general managers that followed Mr Sinclair did not assist continuity.

An early effect of National Bus Company management was the absorption with effect from January 1971 of Stratford-upon-Avon Blue Motors, a subsidiary since 1935. Many believe that Stratford Blue was not absorbed by BMMO during BET ownership as the group liked to use small companies to train its future managers before moving them to larger organisations.

The next outward sign of NBC management was the adoption of white 'National' coach livery for all subsidiaries. This carried a heavy price for operators like Midland Red, however. The extensive goodwill built up by the company was largely swept aside as tours and excursions clients who traditionally travelled Midland Red were deterred by the sight of white express coaches rendered grubby after the slightest shower.

NBC corporate livery also spread to the bus fleet. Initially NBC subsidiaries that traditionally painted their vehicles red were required to choose one of two shades. Midland Red chose the lighter but even that was darker, comparing unfavourably with the traditional. This was soon followed from autumn 1972 by the much brighter poppy red livery with bland lettering.

A large number of Ford single-deckers were taken in between 1970 and 1974 to modernise the ageing rural fleet but, once NBC settled in, Midland Red had little choice in vehicles too. Coaches had to be Leyland Leopards, which suited Midland Red well. The standard NBC double-decker was the Bristol VRT unless requirements were too many, in which case operators with a Leyland tradition could be allocated Atlanteans. Some Leyland Atlanteans were ordered for Midland Red, but economic hard times meant they were reallocated to other NBC operators, and the company never purchased any more double-deckers.

This left the company heavily dependent upon larger single-deckers which, under NBC, meant the dreaded Leyland National. Leyland and NBC had jointly decided that it was a good idea to design a completely new bus and

Left: The crew prepare 5294, numerically the last of the 50 DD11-class Alexander-bodied Daimler Fleetlines delivered in 1963, at Leicester St Margaret's bus station in May 1971. Many D9s and all of the DD11 Fleetlines were built with illuminated panels for advertisements after an initial panel was fitted to D5 3498 while in Works following a serious accident in fog. One trial installation for single-deckers was also fitted to S14 4671. Unfortunately advertisers were unwilling to pay a higher rate, and the illuminated panels were gradually removed from most of these buses. *Malcolm Keeley*

Right: To use up excess stocks, the lower decks of the 1966 batch of DD12-class Daimler Fleetlines had seating upholstered in C5-style moquette, red PVC being standard throughout on subsequent deliveries. The 1966 Fleetlines helped replace, *inter alia*, the LD8 Leylands, of which two of Leamington's allocation, 4048 and 4055, were sold to G&G Coaches. Pictured at Leamington bus station in July 1967, Fleetline 6007 stands ahead of 4048, now dressed in the blue livery of its new owner. *Patrick Kingston*

then build it in a new factory where there was no history or skills of bus manufacture — hence the unreliable National's early nickname of 'Cumberland Dustbin'. Midland Red engineers were understandably appalled. Fortunately, Leyland Leopards were also permitted in dual-purpose form and the company found lots of reasons for buying more. From 1976, dual-purpose Leopards ceased to use a bus shell but assumed the more glamorous guise of a coach design. Nevertheless hundreds of Nationals entered service. In fairness their bodies proved tough and capable of long lives.

Arguably the most traumatic event — and the biggest contraction — was the sale of all services operating entirely within the new West Midlands county (*i.e.* the company's Birmingham and Black Country heartland) to the West Midlands Passenger Transport Executive. The Transport Act 1968 had required Passenger Transport Authorities and Executives to be set up and control all local public transport in their areas, road and rail. Initially WMPTE was handed the assorted municipal buses of the West Midlands but needed an arrangement with the National Bus Company. Unlike in some other PTE areas, NBC was unable to reach an operating agreement with WMPTE and instead sold Midland Red's local West Midlands services. On 3 December 1973 some 413 vehicles and the garages at Dudley, Hartshill, Oldbury, Sheepcote Street, Stourbridge and Sutton Coldfield transferred to WMPTE, together with a large number of the company's experienced platform, engineering and office staff.

Top: CM6T 5673 in the yard behind Birmingham Digbeth garage. *MRK collection*

Above: A service between Birmingham and Northampton was introduced on 31 May 1929. However, Northampton took a parochial view of the licensing powers available to it before the Road Traffic Act 1930, with the result that Midland Red could not get licensed and had to resort to the 'return ticket' strategy: if an operator picked up only those passengers holding return tickets, this did not constitute plying for hire. With effect from 12 April 1930 the route was extended west of Birmingham to Shrewsbury, creating the exceptionally long stage-carriage service, 101 miles long and with around 150 fare stages, familiar to so many readers as the X96. It was obviously a prime route for dual-purpose vehicles such as 5839, seen at Pool Meadow, Coventry, when new in March 1967. This was the first of 10 Leyland Leopard PSU3s with long-window 49-seat bodywork by Willowbrook, the LS20 class. *T. W. Moore*

Left: Introduced in 1967, the 30 BMMO S21 49-seat semi-coach vehicles were designed primarily for light weekday stage-carriage work and weekend coach duties. The first 11 had the established red-and-black livery, but from No 5860 maroon replaced the black. The seats were unusual, being blue and upholstered in PVC — rather sweaty on long journeys. Commencing with the LS20s and the S21s, rear route-number-blind boxes were no longer fitted, and from January 1970 the existing fleet had rear blinds removed and the glass overpainted. The S21s, meanwhile, were followed in 1968 by 37 S22-class 45-seat dual-purpose vehicles intended for longer-distance stage-carriage services and private-hire work, but despite their enhanced quality these were painted in unrelieved red. The S21s and S22s had fixed windows, ventilation being by air drawn through roof scoops and delivered through nozzles above each seat. Here S21 5874 passes through Peterborough bus station in August 1973, by which time the all-red livery had spread. The silver fleetnames applied for a time to coaches and semi-coaches shows up well. *Malcolm Keeley*

Left: The final production run of BMMO-built vehicles comprised 76 S23 service buses with revised glazing incorporating top-sliding ventilators. With Halesowen spreading out in the background, the driver gives 5950 full throttle as it hits the increasing incline from the Fighting Cocks, Romsley. *Brian Tromans / The Transport Museum, Wythall*

Right: The Production Department staff may look cheerful, but this is a very sad working day. The date is 27 February 1970, and the very last BMMO, 5991, is about to leave Central Works. Many later BMMO buses had their bodies completed by Willowbrook or, as in this case, Plaxton. *The Transport Museum, Wythall*

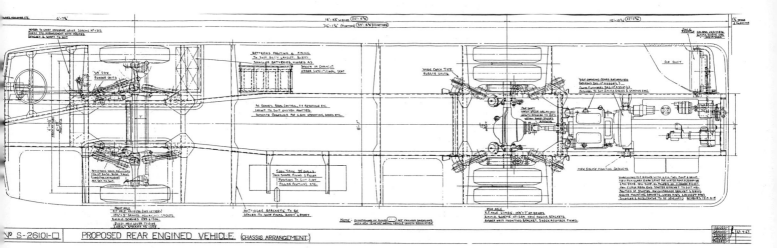

№ S-26101-□   PROPOSED REAR ENGINED VEHICLE. (CHASSIS ARRANGEMENT.)

Above: Chassis arrangement of a proposed BMMO rear-engined single-decker, with BMMO 10.5-litre engine, drawn on 27 September 1967. Work was well advanced on this design to 11- and 12-metre lengths before it was cancelled; indeed, 150 gear-boxes had been ordered from Self-Changing Gears for delivery over three years.

Left: Western SMT's ex-David MacBrayne 1965 Bedford VAS1 with Willowbrook body stands at Rest and be Thankful, the highest point on the A83 between Arrochar and Inverary, as Midland Red 1969 Leopard PSU4A/Plaxton 36-seater 614/ storms by on a Scottish tour in August 1972. This junction has to be one of Britain's least-likely bus termini; the Bedford is waiting to connect with buses on the main road before travelling to Carrick Castle. Midland Red's buses served deeply rural areas but nothing as wild as this! *The Transport Museum, Wythall*

Right: Midland Red's later Alexander-bodied Daimler Fleetlines, the DD13 class, had additional centre exits, which many drivers discouraged passengers from using. The final batch of 33, delivered in 1970/1, also had a revised style of dash panel and other differences. No 6279 stands in Bearwood bus station in August 1971. *The Transport Museum, Wythall*

Right: The Stratford Blue fleet was ancient until its startling transformation between 1948 and 1950. The only postwar acquisitions until then had been eight 1930 Tilling-Stevens B10A2 models with 1935 Eastern Counties 31-seat bodies, bought in 1946 from North Western. This is No 30 (DB 9389). *MRK collection*

Below: Superb sign-writing at Stratford bus station — little chance of vandalism in those days. *BMMO*

Above: Two of the new Stratford Blue Leylands delivered in 1948 in the bus station alongside the Red Lion. No 41 (GUE 247), a PS1 with Northern Coach Builders 34-seat body, is still in existence at Wythall but in need of much money. No 32 (GUE 238) was a PD2 with Leyland's own 56-seat bodywork and as such was direct precursor to Midland Red's LD8 class (3978-4077) of 1952/3. *R. T. Wilson / The Transport Museum, Wythall*

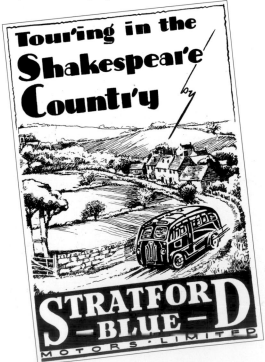

Touring in the
Shakespeare
Country *by*

STRATFORD
BLUE
MOTORS LIMITED

MIDLAND RED · STRATFORD BLUE

ENQUIRIES

BUSES
LEAVE HERE
FOR

ALCESTER · ALDERMINSTER ·
ALVESTON · ASTON-CANTLOW ·
ASTON-SUB-EDGE · BIDFORD ·
BIRMINGHAM · BROADWAY ·
BROMSGROVE · CHIPPING-
CAMPDEN · CHIPPING NORTON ·
COVENTRY · ETTINGTON ·
EVESHAM · HAMPTON LUCY ·
HENLEY · HEREFORD · HINCKLEY ·
HOCKLEY HEATH · ILMINGTON ·
KENILWORTH · KINETON ·
LANGLEY · LEAMINGTON ·
LEDBURY · LEICESTER · LOXLEY ·
MALVERN · MICKLETON ·
NEWBOLD-ON-STOUR · NUNEATON ·
OXFORD · PERSHORE ·
PILLERTON PRIORS · QUINTON ·
REDDITCH · SAINTBURY ·
SHIPSTON-ON-STOUR ·
SHOTTERY · SHIRLEY ·
STRETTON-ON-FOSSE ·
STUDLEY · WARWICK ·
WELFORD · WILLERSEY ·
WOOTTON-WAWEN · WOODSTOCK ·
WORCESTER ·

Right: In later years the backbone of Stratford Blue's many rural services was the Leyland Tiger Cub. This Marshall-bodied 41-seater, 53 (5455 WD), dated from 1962 and was finished to dual-purpose standard. The land adjacent to the Red Lion was then familiar as the loading-point for most of Stratford's bus services. Seen alongside on 14 July 1969 is No 30 (2769 NX), one of three Leyland PD3/4 buses new in 1960 with 73-seat forward-entrance Willowbrook bodywork. *Paul Gray*

Right: After a batch of Northern Counties bodies on new PD3 and overhauled PS2 chassis Stratford Blue reverted to Willowbrook coachwork on its final eight traditional double-deckers, delivered between 1963 and 1966. These were PD3A/1 models, introducing concealed radiators donkeys' years after the parent company had adopted them. Here the Stratford Blue conductor enjoys the attention as No 4 (671 HNX) works Midland Red service 590 out of Pool Meadow, Coventry, on 10 April 1964. *Patrick Kingston*

Right: Stratford Blue's last new double-deckers were three Leyland Atlantean PDR1/1s with 75-seat Northern Counties bodywork, received in 1967. No 11 (NAC 417F) is seen at Leamington bus station in May 1970 alongside S17 5614. Midland Red quickly passed the trio on to fellow NBC subsidiary City of Oxford. *Patrick Kingston*

15 | In the driving seat

Left: Between 1970 and 1974 Midland Red purchased 140 Fords, with Plaxton 45-seat bodies, for rural services. No 6303, passing through the High Town, Bridgnorth, when new, was one of the first batch, delivered with cream bands on the traditional red. *Brian Tromans/ The Transport Museum, Wythall*

Stan Letts has now acquired a driving licence, for buses as well as cars, thanks in particular to his friend Barry Ware, and then to the company's Driving School. Stan, no doubt, would have stayed with Midland Red until retirement. He was not to know that Midland Red would not stay with him.

'Because the summer was now upon us, and the senior drivers were engaged upon better class coach duties, it followed that most driving turns requiring office part-timers like me would be on the bus equivalents of "top-link" routes. This meant a high diet of latest buses like the majestic D9 — surely the attainment of perfection in the classic front-engine/rear-loader layout. Occasionally a duty would come up on a local route, which would mean struggling with a crash-'box D7. This I enjoyed a lot less, but I needed the money!'

The Black Country beckons

'The summer season came to its close, and as the senior drivers returned to ordinary duties part-time driving work

at Bearwood dried up. Then one day, visiting me at my "day job" in the Timetables Office, Hartshill's genial Superintendent appreciated my situation. "We're always short at our garage," he said. "Give us a ring on Thursday, and we'll see if we can fix you up on Saturday."

'He was as good as his word. Out of garage at 10 in the morning, back at 5.30. Thirteen round-trips on the 283 Brierley Hill and Nagersfield Estate shuttle. As I turned up I was dismayed to be greeted by a D7 waiting for me on the garage forecourt.

'Thirteen round-trips, up and down the Black Country hills, round little estate roads, and a reversing manœuvre at the terminus — all with that dreaded crash 'box. My conductor was a cheery young bloke who was quite happy having to navigate his new driver round the complex. They had the same turn for me the following Saturday. Again it was a D7, yet I now realised that the crash-box no longer held any fears for me. I always reckon that it was the Nagersfield Saturday Shopper that finally banished those fears, and indeed from that moment on I would always pick a crash-'box bus if given the choice.'

'Take it away, driver!'

'This was to stand me in good stead one fine Saturday in the summer. Working from Bearwood, I had the privilege of a D9 on the 1pm 192 out of Birmingham all the way to Ludlow. This journey was always a very busy one, often with nearly a fully seated load.

'Midland Red brakes were never the best, but this D9 really needed a big strong chap to lean on the brake pedal to get the thing to slow down. At the stop by the Land Oak on the approach to Kidderminster, the conductor ran down the side of the bus to address me over the bonnet. Smoke was coming into the saloon and I deduced that oil must be getting on to a brake drum. This would account for the smoke, and for the pedal effort needed. The descent into "Kiddy" was negotiated very gingerly indeed!

'I put my problem to the duty foreman at KR garage. "Can't help you, mate," he replied; "got nothin' to give you." I then spotted a forlorn-looking D7 hiding up a corner. "Anything wrong with that?" I asked the chap in the brown cow-gown. "It's roadworthy — you can have it if you must," he replied, whereupon he called over to a

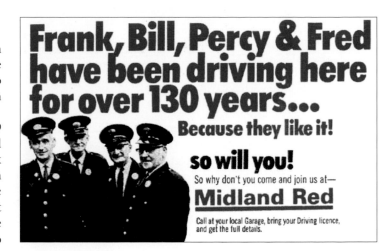

few drivers loitering in the garage. "Here, you lot, come and give that bus a shove!"

'So, propelled by much human-power, the old bus gradually accelerated across the garage, then, with a shudder and a roar, as the foreman let in the clutch, the engine sprang into life. 'Don't stop the b***** thing!' he admonished me.

'It was as I climbed up to set the blinds to "192 Ludlow" that one of the drivers who had participated in this little pantomime sidled up to me. "You ain't thinking of taking this to Ludlow, are you?" he asked. I nodded; "Got no option, have I?" With a "Best of British, mate" and a weary shake of the head he went on his way.

'The passengers were swapped over from the sick D9, and we were now some 25 minutes down. I reasoned that some passengers might have connections to make, so, once on the open road, I leaned hard on the Go pedal. I soon learnt what had caused that driver to issue that dire warning. Once the revs had built up on full throttle the engine kicked up such a clamorous racket that you couldn't hear yourself change your mind.

'It was not until we embarked on the vicious climb out of Hopton Wafers to the Clee Hill summit that another realisation dawned. This two-mile drag, on every other bus I had driven up it, was definitely a bottom-gear slog. What was this ancient D7 doing? Banging away happily in second! We arrived in Ludlow only two minutes late.'

To the Black Country's heart

'In 1971 Midland Red de-centralised its traffic operations. The Timetables Office at Bearwood was closed, and the Schedules personnel (including me) were relocated to their Divisional headquarters. Some had to up-sticks and go to work in Leicester, others to Rugby, others to Worcester. The Birmingham Division lads were re-located to a cubby-hole within the confines of Bearwood garage. I, along with my colleagues of the North West Division, was relocated to the Divisional Office at Dudley.

'This meant that I was grabbed for work there most weekends. I didn't mind at all — the camaraderie at Dudley was every bit as warm as at Bearwood. An office colleague was Alan Broughall, known to many bus enthusiasts

Above: For many years buses and coaches were required to undergo a Certificate of Fitness examination after seven years of service. In their first seven years the CM6T coaches each clocked up around half a million miles, so not surprisingly they were heavily overhauled before being presented for the CoF. The opportunity was taken to facelift some of them, with new destination boxes, fluted side trims and, internally, fresh moquette on the seats. The first Midland Red coach to receive National white livery was CM6T 5652, in June 1972. The earliest repaints perpetuated the silver fleetname used on coaches and dual-purpose vehicles before NBC standardised lettering was imposed. Already grubby after only one month in mid-summer, 5652 approaches Digbeth coach station, Birmingham. *Maurice Collignon*

Right: Conductress Joan Tracey wears full NBC uniform while her driver gets a bit more life out of his traditional BMMO summer dust jacket at Cubbington terminus in July 1975. D9 4851, which had been the first production D9 into passenger service, in January 1960, was coincidentally the first Midland Red bus in NBC poppy red, in August 1972; to accord with new directives on lettering its fleetname had to be hand-painted before stocks of transfers arrived. NBC red was initially unrelieved, but 4851 was blessed with a further repaint, showing here the white band soon permitted by NBC. No 4851 was withdrawn in November 1975, while 14 February 1979 would be the last day for conductors at Leamington.
Patrick Kingston

Left: The short-length LC9-class Leyland Leopard PSU4/Plaxton 36-seat tour coaches delivered in 1966 were downgraded to general coaching duties and upseated to 40 from late 1972. No 5836 wears NBC 'local coach' livery at Bearwood in April 1973. The King's Head is in shot, but other properties have been demolished to permit widening of Hagley Road West. The driver is out of his seat, checking the passenger list.
The Transport Museum, Wythall

Below left: Midland Red continued to take Plaxton-bodied Leyland Leopards for coach work. Plaxton Panorama Elite-bodied PSU3 No 198 dated from 1973 and is seen on a Scottish tour in 1978. *Brian Tromans / The Transport Museum, Wythall*

Right: Among the nice, posh, dual-purpose Leopards moved out of the Black Country garages and retained by Midland Red for its longer stage routes was Oldbury's 6439, here working the very urban 126 route at the King's Head, Bearwood, in April 1973, in which month it was reallocated to Stourbridge. Route 126 and the Oldbury and Stourbridge garages all passed to WMPTE, but 6439, of course, did not, moving initially to Kidderminster. *The Transport Museum, Wythall*

through his photography. He was a very quiet lad but enjoyed doing part-time conducting, and the folk at Dudley would often pair us up with a Saturday shift.

'The Priory Estate in Dudley after pub turning-out time on a Saturday night could be, shall we say, "interesting". The bus that bore the brunt of this revelry was the 10.37pm 281 to Wolverhampton. Most Monday mornings we would be regaled with the near-rioting which took place on this journey, which got so bad that the company had arranged with the Police for it to be regularly accompanied by a Panda car.

'Alan and I reported to Dudley bus station to take over one late-night duty. On studying our running card I nudged Alan. "Here — look what we've got," I said; "the 10.37 281!" The evening passed quietly until half past ten.

'We loaded up our D12 Fleetline in the bus station. Our passengers were by no means quiet, but they didn't seem at all threatening. As we progressed, Alan quietly passed round the bus collecting fares. As he returned to the front of the bus I asked him if he was all right. He simply nodded, meanwhile the passengers' singing was getting more and more raucous — they were clearly very mellow indeed. We arrived at the main stop in Priory Estate to the sound of many boots crashing down the stairs and with many a cheery "G'nigh' driver!" the revellers staggered off the bus and reeled happily home. We gave a thumbs-up sign to the officers in the police car, they drove off, and we finished our shift peacefully.

'So what was all the trouble about? It turned out that the usual "guard" on that duty was a rather officious elderly dragon of a conductress. Instead of turning a deaf ear to the raucous singing she would try to stop it, threatening removal of offenders from the bus. It was this that caused the near rioting. After Alan's experience, she was put onto another roster and the problem just went away.'

A new badge on my hat

'The autumn of 1973 was hectic in the extreme. On 3 December most of the work performed by the Black Country garages would automatically pass to West Midlands PTE — but not all of it. Any service that set foot outside the PTE area would remain with Midland Red. Bearwood garage was to be closed completely and its services in the Black Country would pass to other Black Country garages, while its "country" Midland Red work was taken over by Digbeth. So there was a huge amount of reallocating work between the garages and the workload was immense.

'On 3 December 1973 I said goodbye to the company I had joined in 1948 and became a local government officer under the West Midlands PTE, although I reported to the same office, and sat at the same desk. There was much to-ing and fro-ing at Dudley. All those buses bearing WMPTE stickers would stay, but all those without the stickers would have to go. To accommodate work in the area that was not transferred to the PTE, Midland Red reopened the former garage at Cradley Heath. All the dual-purpose buses were to stay with Midland Red, and Dudley's allocation were destined for Cradley Heath. A few fellow part-timers and I had the task of driving these nice posh buses to their new home.

'I led the convoy, and arrived at Cradley Heath to find all in pitch darkness. Drawing on my time there of many years ago I knew that the entrance was reached down a driveway alongside the garage itself, so I carefully turned my LS20 into the driveway, only to come to an abrupt halt. Nestling invisibly in the shadows thrown by the boundary fence was a mobile compressor unit — and the bus was firmly wedged against it! A quick back up and a word of warning to my fellow drivers, and we drove up to the locked doors.

'Just then a chappie who claimed that he was the new Engineering Superintendent for Cradley Heath drew up in a flap, opened the doors and switched on the lights. His words were not repeatable when he saw the stove-in side panels of the bus I'd brought. By this time the day was drawing to its end, and we made our way back to Dudley. On arrival I asked for an Accident Report Form. I explained about the prang. The response of Dudley's genial Engineering Superintendent was to look at the clock. "It's just gone midnight," he said. "That's no longer our problem!"

16 | Working for the new regime

Midland Red buses were still to be seen in Birmingham on services to points outside what became West Midlands County in April 1974, but the company was left with a territory with a distinctly rural emphasis. Support for rural services rested with county councils whose attitudes to public transport were to vary widely. The loss of the Birmingham operations was reflected when, in March 1974, the official title was changed to the Midland Red Omnibus Company Limited.

Some of the £3.6 million received from the West Midlands PTE was used to purchase other operators, but this could never replace the lost urban core of profitable routes. Notable independent firms taken over around this time were Green Bus of Rugeley in 1973, Harper Bros of Heath Hayes in 1974 and the bus operations of the Shropshire Omnibus Association Ltd in 1978.

Harper Bros was the biggest independent operator in Staffordshire and an attractive proposition. Midland Red invested in a new garage at Cannock to handle the increased operations in that area and allow Cradley Heath to be closed again. The allocation of 78 buses upon opening in 1977 made Cannock the largest garage on the system.

The Shropshire Omnibus Association takeover enabled Midland Red entirely to restructure services in the Telford and Wellington areas. No buses were acquired, and Midland Red allocated a fleet of new Leyland Nationals to Wellington garage to operate the new network.

Left: The last vehicle to enter service with Stratford Blue, in 1970, proved to have a long life with Midland Red, despite being non-standard, with Alexander coachwork on its Leyland Leopard chassis. Originally a coach, Midland Red 2036 (XNX 136H) was gradually relegated in status, finally being painted in bus livery. In August 1978 it wore 'local coach' livery as it climbed the hill into Cotteridge, Birmingham, from King's Norton. It is now preserved in Stratford Blue colours. *The Transport Museum, Wythall*

Right: This 1972 Bedford YRQ with Duple coach body was acquired from Cooper of Oakengates in 1973. No 2147 (XUX 558K) later worked bus services from Heath Hayes garage, being seen here preparing for the six-minute run to Gorsey Lane from Cannock bus station. *Paul Roberts*

Staff employed by these smaller operators found many changes followed their absorption into Midland Red. **Paul Roberts**, having worked part-time with Harpers from 1969, made the momentous decision in 1973 to become full-time, only to discover a few weeks later that he was about to be employed by Midland Red.

'Working for different bus companies throws up unexpected challenges. One such problem, probably not appreciated by many people outside the industry, is adapting to a different vocabulary. Instead of being sent out in the morning by an inspector, we would be dealt with by a "despatch clerk"; I would no longer be on a spare or standby shift but would be on "show-up", and, if my bus was faulty, it would be attended to by an "engineer", not a mechanic!

'The early period at Heath Hayes, now garage No 35, saw little change, but once it was fully owned by Midland Red many things began to alter. The first difference at the start of a shift was the signing-on procedure. The concept of just wandering in and signing on was new to us all, as a good solid old-fashioned clocking-on machine used to greet the crews previously. It was less forgiving than a real live duty inspector (or was it?), but it saved having to fill in time sheets, a new and unwanted chore bestowed on us by the new regime. Previously we would next go to a large shelf to untangle one of many Setright Speed machines from an untidy pile thrown there by crews on the previous night. The plan was to get one with an easy-to-operate release catch, nicely turning dials and a freely spinning handle, which made the shift much easier. There was no such choice under Midland Red. For the first time Setrights were issued from the despatch office to drivers/conductors, the machine having had its closing numbers checked by the office staff — something Harpers had always been

happy to let the platform staff do. Also the old hardboard running boards were replaced with big metal ones specifically designed to fit into brackets provided on all Midland Red buses.

'Fare collection had been the domain of the roving conductor until the late 1960s, when Harpers began to introduce driver-only operation using a number of systems. One was the issue of a Setright Speed ticket by the driver from a hand-held machine. This would be kept somewhere in the cab area whilst driving between stops (under the driver's seat, on the dashboard or on top of the engine cover if a Bedford was being used). One-man operation frequently involved the use of coaches fitted with a manual door and the driver was kept fit by leaping in and out of his seat to open and close it. Occasionally a helpful passenger would come to his rescue thankfully eliminating the acrobatics over the engine cover and gear lever etc. The next phase saw the conversion of two Burlingham Seagull-bodied Leyland Royal Tigers, Nos 22 and 50. They had already been modified for stage-carriage work with ugly flat bus fronts and two-piece glider doors, but in their latter years they acquired Setright stands and state of the art cash-vaults, as used by the neighbouring WMPTE on its fleet. This meant that no change could be given to the passengers who were expected to tender the exact fare. This made cash collection extremely quick and easy for the driver.

'The final development was the delivery of a pair of ECW-bodied Daimler Fleetline CRL6s, which eventually became Nos 2233/4, that came equipped with full Autofare equipment, again including cash-vaults. I often drove these two buses in one-man mode on Sundays and late shifts. Passengers soon became used to them and loading was quick and easy. As soon as Midland Red took over, this ticket system was removed, and all the rear-engined double-deckers were converted to the MROC standard for ticket issuing. This involved a Setright Speed mounted on an electric power pack and cash trays in the cab. These

Left: Acquired from Green Bus of Rugeley, 1972 Seddon Pennine IV 2154 (FRF 762K) received NBC poppy-red livery but was not retained for long. *Alan D. Broughall*

Left: A Harpers ex-London RTL shows off its new Midland Red Omnibus Co legal lettering while LS18 Leopard 5186 of the incoming regime tries Heath Hayes yard for size. *Paul Roberts*

Right: The 'ON HIRE TO MIDLAND RED' sticker in the windscreen is the only indication that this is a Midland Red rather than a Harper picture as ex-London RTL KXW 284, now officially Midland Red 2204, pulls away from Heath Hayes yard. *Paul Roberts*

had to be hurriedly emptied at the end of each period of duty before handing over to a relief driver. This was seen by many of the staff at that time as a retrograde step; however, Arriva Midlands, the successor to much of Midland Red, still uses the same cash system in the 21st century!

'Talking of cash — at the end of the day the conductor had to pay in his takings. At Harpers, crews on late shift would bag-up their money and take it across from the mess room to the back of the shop, where Albert Harper would be waiting in the office and, in cold weather, warming himself by the open fire. After a brief chat he would take the money, throw it in a cupboard near the fireplace, close the door, turn the key, and that was it. Strange to say, Midland Red did not favour this particular brand of home-made security. When they took over the garage it would only be a couple of years before Cannock opened so it was not worth installing a drop-safe. A cashier was now kept on duty until the end of service in order to accept the revenue. It was then secured in a conventional safe.

'Harpers' cash seemed to find its way to the bank with no assistance from the road staff. Midland Red favoured taking the daily takings to the Midland Bank at Hednesford, two miles from Heath Hayes, using as much muscle as could be mustered from its own ranks on the day. Every morning a "show-up" driver would fetch a bus, preferably a Fleetline, but sometimes a Leyland PD2 or PD3 from the bus park, and bring it across to the garage. Any other spare staff, many off-duty crews being bribed with the promise of an extra hour's pay, would then assist. The cash was stashed in locked trolleys, resembling laundry baskets on castors, and the heavy cargo of change was heaved aboard the bus ready to be transported with its amiable throng of impromptu security guards laughing and joking, literally, all the way to the bank. On arrival the staff would form

two columns from the bus into the bank in the manner of a guard of honour. The valuable load would then be trundled across the footpath and into safe custody. This procedure was repeated daily at Midland Red garages throughout the Midlands (including Cannock, when it opened) and I certainly never heard of anybody attempting to make off with the money.

'Another feature, which appealed to all the enthusiast drivers, was the daily run to the hallowed Central Works at Edgbaston. This sacred ground had hitherto been almost impenetrable to anyone not connected with Midland Red. Now a daily delivery run was introduced to and from the works. Heath Hayes received a BMC FG lorry and yet again it fell to the "show-up" drivers to transport the mixed cargo of expired or re-conditioned engines and gearboxes, spare parts, seats, etc. Unloading and loading was done by the staff at Central Works whilst the lorry driver went for a cuppa or, in my case, a sneak round all the restricted areas to see what gems of vehicles were lurking in the secret corners of the premises. This was only four years after the last new BMMO bus had emerged and much time was spent maintaining its home-produced products.

'Harpers, unlike many independent operators, had issued uniforms to all of its staff, including part-timers. This was very heavy blue serge, not unlike that of Midland Red, only with green piping. By the time the company had been taken over the NBC had issued its new standard uniform, including the flamboyant American-style "three-penny bit" caps. Staff at Heath Hayes had previously been issued with uniforms from a cupboard at the back of the Traffic Office. Midland Red made it a lot more exciting by centralising its uniform stores at Central Works. This required a personal visit for measuring and fitting — another excuse for an illicit wander round! One surprising feature, which made it very difficult to keep the NBC mid-blue uniform clean and

fresh was the requirement for drivers to refuel their own buses at the end of a shift. Handling the fuel nozzle, and splash-backs from narrow-necked fuel pipes on the buses, often conspired to leave a freshly cleaned uniform smelling like a garage forecourt. Harpers, with just 50 vehicles, had an employee designated to re-fuel the buses and this practice continued until Heath Hayes was closed. As soon as Cannock opened, Midland Red imposed its self-fuelling policy on drivers — something Health & Safety rules would eventually outlaw.

'In the early takeover days Harpers' own vehicles were regular visitors to Central Works, for repainting. I remember having a look round one day and seeing the last PD3, 2223, having its destination box converted to the standard Midland Red layout. Although it was with mixed feelings that we lost the unusual green and cream livery there was a definite buzz on seeing the pristine result of a Central Works repaint. It has to be remembered that in the early stages we did not know if the Titans would survive with their new owners. I also remember going to fetch a freshly repainted Bedford SB5 coach, resplendent in its National white livery. A more sedate journey home than usual ensued, knowing that any battle scars could only be put down to one person — me! Soon afterwards, I was driving the same coach on a colliery contract service. The miners, at this time, were unused to seeing the famous white livery on their route, but most Midland folk were aware of the reputation of BMMO's coaches for high-speed motorway running. One passenger sat alongside me as the under-powered Bedford made its usual sedate progress towards West Cannock No 5 Colliery. After a few minutes' contemplation he leaned across and said: "Cor, these Midland Red coaches don't half go well," being blissfully unaware that it was the same vehicle that had been taking him to work for the past four years.

'The biggest change for the driving staff was getting to grips with Midland Red buses. To an enthusiast, such as myself, it was a major thrill to have such vehicles in the fleet but to many of the drivers it was just an unnecessary chore re-adjusting to the delights of crash-box S16s. Harpers had operated eight RTLs and RTs, which at 26ft x 7ft 6in were a lot easier to drive through various narrow estate roads than the 36ft x 8ft 2in leviathans that Midland Red sent to replace them. Also the London Transport-designed double-deckers had light, easy-to-operate pre-select gearboxes. No prizes for guessing which ones were preferred by the drivers. Surprisingly several of these ageing double-deckers stayed in service with Midland Red, often working all day long rather than the peak hours they were previously used to. This was so that they could cover for the intensive repaint programme, which was required to stamp the new corporate identity on the more modern members of the fleet. The RTs and RTLs did carry Midland Red Omnibus Co Ltd legal lettering but never had any other identity change. Midland Red added 2,200 to the Harper fleet number but only the newer vehicles, with a long-term future, actually displayed them.

'The Heath Hayes engineers were probably none too pleased to have BMMO-built buses appear on site although it was, of course, almost inevitable at that time. A new Midland Red-trained engineering superintendent was drafted in, presumably to help introduce the company's working ways to Heath Hayes and to bring some first-hand knowledge of the idiosyncrasies of the BMMO-built buses. We were, on takeover, allocated a number of LS18 buses and LS20 dual-purpose vehicles, both based on Leyland Leopard chassis, a type that already featured in the Harpers fleet. The buses were cold and draughty and had big clunky Westinghouse gear levers; the DPs were also a bit rattly but very fast (and, for the passengers, very

comfortable), and I enjoyed driving both types of vehicle. Their iconic BET-style bodywork gave them a real "big company" feel.

'In fairness to Midland Red, we were allocated some of the last production run of BMMO single-deckers. These brought home to us the high quality of the output from Carlyle Road. They had smooth-running, powerful 10.5-litre engines, semi-automatic gearboxes, with miniature electronically controlled gear levers mounted on the steering column, and light but positive steering. As some of our routes had long inter-urban sections these buses were ideally suited to these services and were popular with the drivers.

At the other end of the spectrum we were also seen, by the powers-that-be, as a rural garage and were allocated some of the dreaded Fords. On the plus side they had light and airy Plaxton bodies and were equipped with power-assisted steering (still a rarity at that time). On the minus side they were hot and noisy for the driver, having the engine alongside. Their manual synchromesh gearboxes were far less positive than the constant-mesh S16s', and gear selection was often a matter of luck, rather than judgement, especially on the final batch, which had six forward gears. Ultra sensitive brakes also meant that in wet weather, when lightly laden, their skating antics would have done credit to Torvill and Dean. This was not so funny when you were in the hot seat and carrying a precious cargo of real people. They were some of the newest buses in the fleet, but I do not recall any driver actually liking them.

'Another advantage to enthusiast drivers was the system of re-allocating buses to different garages. Many of the vehicle swaps were left to the "show-ups", and I enjoyed several Midland Red-sponsored one-man excursions whilst engaged in such operations. Sometimes three-way swaps

would lead to driving interesting buses from other garages. This sort of trip involved such itineraries as "Take bus 'A' to Central Works, pick up bus 'B' and take it to Leicester Southgate and then bring bus 'C' back to Heath Hayes". Meandering through the countryside was an absolute delight — every PSV driver knows that an empty bus is a happy bus! I am sure that the Vehicle Allocation Officer at Midland House must have had my wellbeing in mind when designing such itineraries.

'The reader may be getting the impression that every day was a holiday. This was not so — crews worked hard carrying loads which would be unheard of in today's car-orientated society. Peak-hour services on the trunk route from Cannock to Birmingham carried up to four relief buses, all full, and very few passengers had any form of season ticket. The coming of Midland Red meant that we drivers found our weekly wage packet almost doubled but, unfortunately, within a year of the change, passengers were paying hugely increased fares.

'Some of the Harper family continued in employment with Midland Red along with their erstwhile staff, but others, particularly the patriarchal figure of Albert Harper, took the opportunity to retire. This was bound to have an effect on the day-to-day feel at the garage, but some of his influence continued whilst the Midland Red working practices gradually took over.

'The biggest change of all came in 1977, when the whole operation moved to a brand-new garage at Delta Way, Cannock, and the integration process was completed for the ex-Harpers crews. These premises also became home to the band of nomadic drivers and staff who had been allocated to the temporarily reopened Cradley Heath garage, base for the recently acquired ex-Wolverhampton Corporation country services part-exchanged in the big deal with WMPTE. Many of these Black Country staff were dyed-in-the-wool BMMO employees. Much friendly rivalry continued between the two groups of staff, particularly with the Heath Hayes men trying to convince the others as to the superiority of their former company. But the old atmosphere finally expired, crew operations ceased, and most of the conductors were re-trained as drivers or took redundancy.

'This was an era of takeovers for MROC, and, as the companies fell, the staff who wished to remain in service with their new employer were sent off to Central Works for re-training, Midland Red style. Harpers staff was exempt from this procedure. Most drivers were involved in stage-carriage, contract and summer express services, and also some were involved with private hires, excursions and tours. It would have been a monumental task to send such a large workforce on the appropriate courses, and so the decision was taken to accept our Harpers service as contributory to that of Midland Red, *e.g.* a "twenty-year" man would be deemed to have worked that length of time for Midland Red. More importantly to me, as a 25-year-old "coach driver", status was left intact, so this title was carried over to a company where most drivers had to reach their senior years before being allowed even to touch a coach. When I took C9 5834 to Scotland on a week-long holiday tour, I was probably the youngest Midland Red driver ever to do so. Incidentally the organiser of this tour was Mary Harper, who continued to use the services of her known and established drivers for several years to come.

'Much as I enjoyed stage-carriage service, particularly when on two-man crew work, I always wanted to drive long-distance trips. Harpers gave its inexperienced drivers a chance to sample coach driving by sending the rookie as second man on seaside express services. These were operated every Saturday throughout the season. Such services readily fitted in with the Midland Red way of working. I soon became acquainted with routes to Pwllheli, Llandudno, Weymouth and Bournemouth. The experienced driver would, in most cases, show the new driver various ways of making the job work more efficiently and show him the quickest routes and shortcuts (even though the route was strictly laid down in the licence!). Tickets were hand-written by the agents and, after the takeover, included a service number. One Saturday a driver stopped for his break at Chirk, just over the Welsh border on the A5, and a passenger said to him: "This is the prettiest journey we have ever made going to Bournemouth." The driver retorted: "That's because we are going to Barmouth!" On checking the ticket he discovered that it had been made out to "B'mouth". This was an abbreviation used by the agents for both resorts, so it was useful having a service number too. It was a shame that the driver didn't actually look at it!

'Not long after becoming part of the NBC, I took a Bedford SB5 on the express service to Rhyl. On the way back, with a full load of returning holidaymakers, my coach spectacularly expired with a seized engine. The location

was a few miles south of Chester, and a major advantage of 'large group' membership became apparent. Instead of waiting for my home garage to make a 100-mile journey to assist, they could contact Crosville, just a few miles away, which would come to my rescue. This it did, in fine style, providing me with a Bristol MW bus as a replacement. It was quite a surprise to see the errant Bedford being towed into Heath Hayes garage the next day behind a BMMO cut-down D7 towing wagon. The MW was to be the first of many interesting "foreign" vehicles that I would drive in years to come. These included a Royal Blue Bristol RE and an LH, an Eastern Scottish Plaxton-bodied Seddon Pennine VII and, when no coach was available in Bedford, a United Counties Bristol VR double-decker.

'This delight backfired on me one day. As my Bedford struggled to ascend the escarpment from Petersfield towards Chichester I started to have visions of rugged Southdown Leyland Leopards. Chichester happily replaced my coach for the journey to Brighton … but with a dreaded Duple-bodied Ford. I'd forgotten that Southdown had taken a number of them into stock! I have never been so pleased to see a Bedford as when I returned to my repaired coach at Chichester.

'The coming of Midland Red also affected our social lives. Harpers had provided its employees with a Social (Temperance) Club where a few events were staged. For an independent operator, this was actually an unusual provision. Any competitions were held locally, with minor tournaments being staged against local pubs and clubs. When Midland Red took over, a whole new family of friends was opened up to us. Inter-garage sporting events were arranged annually on a divisional basis, with winners playing off semi-finals and finals in other areas. We were in the North West Division and competed against Stafford, Wellington, and Shrewsbury. The company provided a bus,

free of charge, as long as one of the team drove it on a volunteer basis. Even within the same division, Shrewsbury was 30 miles away and an enjoyable trip out, particularly in the summer. We came top in a pub-games competition and went to a play-off at Coalville. Having won this, we moved on to a Grand Final at Leamington Midland Red Sports and Social Club. I cannot remember the outcome, but it was a good way for the company to encourage its widespread employees to communicate with each other.

'This camaraderie only failed us once. Our popular engineering superintendent suggested that a good way of integrating platform, engineering and office staff would be a men's night out — there were very few women on the payroll at that time. This was duly arranged at Twycross

Country Club, just over the county border, in Leicestershire. On the night in question over 50 staff climbed aboard a coach and embarked on their night of 'adult entertainment'. Some time after 10.30pm, the hour in those days when ordinary pubs closed, the lights came on and the Keystone Cops apparently quick-marched into the venue and onto the stage. Alas, they were actually the Leicestershire Constabulary raiding the club for selling alcoholic drinks to non-members after normal hours. The sting in the tail was that Midland Red, Leicester, provided the police transport. Fortunately all charges were eventually dropped, a second excursion to Market Bosworth Magistrates Court was avoided, and diplomatic relations were restored between Heath Hayes and Leicester!'

Above: NBC white coach livery could look well on a fine day. On the left of this line-up of Leyland Leopards at Twycross Zoo is 2264 (SBF 218J), an ex-Harpers manual-gearbox version of 1970, with Plaxton coachwork. The other three have semi-automatic gearboxes and Duple bodies. LC7s 5800 and 5793, new to Midland Red in 1965, flank ex-Harpers 2255 (MRF 420L), new in 1972. *Paul Roberts*

Left: Harper Bros had two ECW-bodied Fleetlines and two more on order at the time of takeover. Finally delivered direct to Midland Red in 1976, forming the D14 class, these latter would be the last new double-deckers received by the company. Appropriately they were allocated to Heath Hayes. No 439 loads in Carrs Lane, Birmingham, in May 1976.
The Transport Museum, Wythall

Red sunset | 17

A rather surprising reorganisation in December 1978 converted the last surviving garage in the Birmingham area, Digbeth, into a coach unit. All bus duties were transferred to garages further afield while, apart from a few vehicles at Cannock and Leicester, all coaches were concentrated at Digbeth. The garage also received the services, tours and contracts of the Midland garages of National Travel (West). The centralisation of coach work meant that Digbeth busmen found themselves as coach drivers, a different job entirely requiring different people skills, while senior men at other garages lost the premier coaching work.

Despite NBC, the innovative spirit within Midland Red survived. Surveys indicated that smaller buses had a niche. The usual answer was to buy van-based vehicles like the Ford Transit, but bus operators then were concerned that they would not be tough enough for stop-start bus work. A number of the early 1970s Ford buses were shortened by the company at Central Works, giving just a bit of the excitement of the old days!

Surveys, computer analysis and marketing revolved around the company's pioneering Market Analysis Project. The principle of MAP was that each garage should be able

Left: This World War 2 AEC Matador recovery vehicle, acquired from the military in 1947, was rebuilt in 1962 and, with its C5 windscreen, became something of a cult vehicle, being for many years resident at Digbeth. Painted white after rebuilding, that it might be more easily seen, it was repainted yellow when this became the accepted colour for maximum visibility. It is pictured on standby duty at the National Exhibition Centre during the October 1978 Motor Show. *Malcolm Keeley*

Right: Engineers can produce some interesting vehicles when left to their own devices. LS18 Leopard 5242 was withdrawn with accident damage in 1975 and converted to a towing truck, as seen here at Central Works. *The Transport Museum, Wythall*

Above: The *Staff Bulletin* remarked that personnel underwent special courses of instruction on maintenance procedures for the Leyland National, which had numerous unusual features. This comment was not applied to the cheap-and-cheerful Fords that arrived around the same time, which were simpler and, no doubt, more reliable. Midland Red favoured the longer, single-door version of the National. No 749, a 1979 delivery, is seen when new. *Brian Tromans / The Transport Museum, Wythall*

Right: Dual-purpose Leopards continued to be purchased for longer bus services, a total of 100 with Marshall bodies arriving in 'local coach' livery in 1973/4. Among these was 353, pictured travelling through Belbroughton. *Brian Tromans / The Transport Museum, Wythall*

Left: Dual-purpose Leopards became more glamorous from 1976, when examples with Plaxton Supreme bodywork — 'Bus Grant' versions of coaches — were introduced. Having just completed another journey along the M5 from Birmingham on 1 April 1976, 457 grins at the photographer, albeit out-grinned this April Fool's Day by BMMO S21 5863. The location is Worcester's former bus station in Newport Street, occasionally washed down and put out of use by the River Severn in flood, certainly no joke. *The Transport Museum, Wythall*

Left: In the van (if you'll pardon the expression) of minibuses were five 1974 Ford Transits with 16-seat conversions by Dormobile, purchased from London Country in 1977. Midland Red, still issuing class designations, styled them M1. No 2121 awaits its next duty at Evesham on 4 July 1978. *The Transport Museum, Wythall*

Right: Midland Red could see the benefit of small buses for rural routes but was concerned that van conversions would not be tough enough. It therefore shortened several Ford 45-seaters upon overhaul for recertification after seven years' service. Some of the resulting 27-seat 'midibuses' were supplied to other NBC companies. In this view from September 1978 Hereford boasts a flock of Fords, including shortened 6392, with 'Wandaward' local identity. *The Transport Museum, Wythall*

to support itself financially, with the network being slimmed until break-even was achieved. Routes were revised to meet the needs of as many passengers as possible. County councils could add to this basic network by providing financial support. MAP eventually spread throughout the NBC empire and into Scotland, but it started life with Midland Red. It did have the serious deficiency of only researching the needs of existing passengers and dispensed with those who could not be handled within the minimum number of vehicles and drivers. It paid minimal attention to seeking out new clientele which household-based surveys would have discovered. MAP was thus a recipe for contraction and Midland Red shrank and shrank.

By 1981 the whole of the Midland Red system had received the MAP treatment and was divided into handy compartments, each with an individual marketing name. The only exception was Leicester, where services in the city were shared with the City Transport. The fleet size had slumped to around 900 vehicles, half the total of 20 years previous. NBC had a number of subsidiaries in a similar

condition, each with excess headquarters and works facilities. Midland Red, the company with a hole in the middle after the sale to West Midlands PTE, was an easy target for division.

The announcement came in February 1981 that the company would be divided up and the portions, all still to use the Midland Red fleetname, placed under the care of adjacent NBC companies. Midland House and Carlyle Works staff were given notice of redundancy to take effect after 5 September. The company was split as planned on 6 September 1981 with five new operating companies receiving management assistance from other NBC subsidiaries:

New company	Base	Assisted by
Midland Red (Express) Ltd	Digbeth	Bristol
Midland Red (East) Ltd	Leicester	Trent
Midland Red (North) Ltd	Cannock	Potteries
Midland Red (South) Ltd	Rugby	United Counties
Midland Red (West) Ltd	Worcester	Bristol

Many Midland House employees managed to find positions with the new companies, but by no means all. The fine building remained with the NBC, however, which moved in some of its own staff from elsewhere. Carlyle Road 'Central' Works was saved but its future remained under review. 'Carlyle Works' became a trading name and had to break even to survive. Its spare capacity was taken up by attracting outside jobs, competing commercially for private coach and road freight vehicle overhauls and repairs.

The creation of the five companies seemed an interim arrangement prior to total absorption by the old-established undertakings providing back-up facilities. This possibility quickly receded as the new companies imposed their own identities with imaginative publicity and liveries, the latter the first breaks anywhere from the rigorously imposed NBC directive. However, it required a major mental readjustment to realise that the new companies were not related, except as NBC subsidiaries, and that they could be in competition with each other.

This was the structure as the Conservative Government privatised the NBC subsidiaries and, on 26 October 1986, introduced deregulation. Co-operation between companies was now seen as anti-competitive.

The five operating companies passed to separate buyers, although Midland Red (Express), renamed Midland Red Coaches, soon passed into the same hands as West and was later absorbed. Mergers caused each company to change hands several times. Some owners clearly intended to develop their businesses, while others appeared to want to do nothing but strip out costs. Within 20 years much of the operating industry had re-grouped into a few large concerns, imposing their own corporate liveries. The National Express Group dominated the West Midlands heartland. Stagecoach had South, passing the Banbury operations to its Oxford subsidiary. West had become First Wyvern and merged with First operations in Leicester and — 80 years after BMMO showed interest there — Northampton. North and East were back together under Arriva.

Will, at some time, the story turn full circle, and an accountant or politician declare that it would be much more sensible if one big bus company radiated from Britain's second city? The marketeer alongside would then declare a need to break away from the existing liveries and adopt the brightest in the colour palette. Perchance Midland Red is not dead but sleeping!

Left: In 1979 Midland Red purchased several elderly Leyland Atlantean and Daimler Fleetline double-deckers from Potteries, but only one entered service. Atlantean 2910 of 1962 had a Weymann semi-lowbridge body and thus challenged 4844's claim as Midland Red's only lowbridge double-decker. It is seen waiting at St Margaret's bus station, Leicester, on 14 April 1979. *Malcolm Keeley*

Right: No 832 was delivered before the September 1981 split but did not enter service until after it. An early Leyland Tiger TRCTL11 with Plaxton Supreme coachwork, it was therefore a Midland Red (Express) vehicle when photographed in Cardiff in April 1982. The coachbuilder soon adopted its Paramount design, so the Tiger/ Supreme combination remained something of a rarity. *Malcolm Keeley*